Pupy Love

By

Ric Hart

**Grosvenor House
Publishing Limited**

This book is published by
Grosvenor House Publishing Ltd
Link House
140 The Broadway, Tolworth, Surrey, KT6 7HT.
www.grosvenorhousepublishing.co.uk

A CIP record for this book
is available from the British Library

ISBN 978-1-83975-467-8

www.jadehartpupylove.co.uk
Insta - @hugoandricstravels / @richardhart786
Facebook - Ric Hart / Jade Hart Pupy Love
You Tube - jadehartpupylove

Ric and Jades Love Story

Valentine's Weekend One
to Remember 2002

The alarm went off, and it was Friday morning around 7.30 after a heavy drinking session in the club at Karisma, Doncaster the night before, tuning into 50 Cent in the club with my Evisu denim jacket on. Did I have my shades on in the club? I hope not!! What did I do? Who did I kiss? *I hope I didn't make a fool of myself* came to mind. Must have got in about 2am but still had the energy to bounce out of bed and get my sixth form tie on and get ready for school.

My brother Jay was pretty cool at this time as he had a Fiesta, so off we went heading for school with Ja Rule "Livin' It Up" pumping out. The beatbox system was loud, and everyone always knew we were near due to the amps in the back of Jay's car. I walked into the common room to speak to a few of my pals "What went down last night, boys? Messy night" and still tasting the grogs from Yates pub on my tongue... good job I didn't hit the diesel hard as wouldn't have got up period.

I had a business studies class around 10am and having already planned ahead with my work, I decided to sack off my lesson and head for Maccy D's with the boys to chat about girls girls girls over a dirty double sausage and egg McMuffin, with BBQ sauce always. Having headed back to school, I decided to play some cards with the lads for some money and won a few quid.

Midday struck, and I had missed my lesson and wanted to just head home, so that's what I did. At this time, I was living in Bentley, Doncaster, where I grew up from the age of 11. Dad had a very busy life, which meant I had lots of independence at a young age, and to be honest, it was bloody awesome. My parents broke up when I was around 10, and my dad stayed in the family home, and Mum lived near town, so wasn't too far away.

It was around 2.30pm, and I just hit the deck at home and must have slept for three hours. My alarm went off and also messages flying in from some pals from Hallcross School at the time as it was my work pal at Morrisons' birthday, his 18th, and I had totally forgotten but was sat at home thinking *Do I go or not?* So, I just said, *Sack it; let's go and live it for Friday night out in Wakefield.* Little did I know that this night would change and shape the rest of my life forever.

Off we went on the minibus to Wakefield, and I had an Irn-Bru in my hand, trying to get the feeling again and recharge for Wakey. I remember going into a sports bar and hitting the shots with the lads, and then we headed for a club called IKON. At this point I was feeling OK and ready for a good dance and to see if I could pull a fitty. I remember walking into the club, so I must have been pretty sober at this point, always recall the narrow lane leading into IKON, but the night was booming, and they also had an R&B room which I loved so there I headed.

I was stood at the bar in the R&B room, and I remember looking over my shoulder to see a gorgeous brunette looking over at me, leant against the wall with a wicked blue in her hand. We kept making eye contact, which made me feel I just wanted to go over to her. I remember dancing before we headed to the bar where I said with cheek, "So are you going to buy me a vodka Red Bull then?"

She grinned and thought this guy has lots of confidence. I asked her for her name, and she replied, "I'm called Michelle." The night went on where we found ourselves dancing together and also we kissed, which was amazing, and I just thought, *Wow, this girl is just out of this world stunning and amazing.*

We stumbled out the club with myself heading for the minibus back to Doncaster, and I had got Michelle's number, and we were talking all the way to 5am up to when she said the milkman has arrived. She then told me her real name was Jade Michelle Hazelgrave.

I was certainly privileged to be told her real name, and it made me feel like she must like me as she never told anyone her real name at that time, so she said.

The day after Jade got the Wakefield 485 bus over to Bentley, which took around an hour to come to my house, and what was officially like our first date but felt like we had known each other ages. It also just felt right and amazing at all levels. I remember she had her blue knitted jumper on and skin-tight jeans, slipping into a size 6 back then. We spent all day just lying next to each other and staring into each other's eyes. I think I even told her she is definitely someone I could fall in love with and she's the one, but I was 18 years old – we just said what we thought and did what we wanted, end of, without a worry or concern in the world, and I had heaps of confidence. So that was that; me and Jade started seeing much more of each other during spring 2002.

Our first Official date was at Ackworth Balti House which was effectively a garage with a room and kitchen attached to it, and we had an Indian, Jade just loved a good Chicken Korma and I had the hottest thing on the menu no doubt. I remember this day so clearly, I wasn't too impressed with the food and Jade was saying please don't complain, lol. Anyway I didn't and we just stared into each others eyes over a coke and curry.

Our relationship grew over the following two to three months where we knew everything about each other. Jade always found it fascinating I have Indian in me and was born in Germany, which to be fair is different. I always used to do this funny Indian accent to her, and she just giggled with that look when you look at someone and you're falling for them.

We started spending most days together and also socialising loads with groups of friends and each other. I would even pay my friends and brother £5 each time to go and pick Jade up from her house and even drop her off. £10 back then was a four-hour working shift done at my workplace Morrisons, but it was all worth every penny. I remember going to Jade's Gothic ball 2002 where she had an amazing purple dress on and I had my grey suit on, she had curled her hair, and we were in love. We danced the night away. Our proms were on the same night, so we went to Jade's first and then got a pal to drive us to Doncaster and then we went to my ball which was at the Danum Hotel in Doncaster. We only stayed at mine for 20 minutes as was just getting some boys together to head out in Donny; this was a night to remember. Myself and Jade were very popular as teenagers, we just had lots of confidence, and I have to say we both looked pretty good as well. Most were either jealous or intimidated, but I guess that wasn't our problem, we were certainly embracing and loving life together at 18 years old. I was a very sporty kid in my younger years, having won the South Yorks' karate championship, and also had a great football career as a young lad playing with some top lads who some made it as professional footballers. I guess when you get a taste of success, it really does something for your inner confidence. Me and Jade both had this big time, Jade was creative and had a special way with people, and I knew she was destined for amazing things.

I remember working at Morrisons three days a week earning £2.38 per hour stacking the toilet roll aisle, this makes me laugh writing this now as we are in a pandemic due to Covid-19 and everyone has taken all the bog roll off the shelves; I wouldn't have let that happen, lol. I would have got the job at McDonald's but interviewed badly and, instead, my brother got the job there. But most importantly, I was working and earning and standing on my own two feet at 16, relying on myself. I didn't get the job at McDonald's as they asked, "If a customer came back with a cold burger, what would you say?" My response was, "Eat it, pal." Good job I didn't get the job.

I always remember Jade when she was 17 in her pigtails coming to my house where we would have ice lollies and laugh and kiss constantly. Jade came over one afternoon, and the family dog Madonna was being quite naughty as usual, and I was saying to Jade how much I just loved puppies at the time. I turned to her and said, "You can be my Pupy." She turned to me and said, "Well, you can also be my Pupy," and that was that we agreed to be each other's puppies. From that point onwards, we called each other Pupy but had to be mindful of not doing it in public.

I remember Jade's parents were very strict in terms of me sleeping over, and if I did, I would have to sleep in the spare room, which I got totally and looking back now I would have been the exact same. One night we had gone out drinking, and we ended up sleeping together in her bedroom (not literally). Morning struck, and Jade's mum shouted her and was heading for her bedroom, so I hid under the quilt as Jade and her mum were having a full-on conversation about what to have for breakfast as they always made full English on Saturdays and Sunday, which tasted amazing thanks to John (Jade's dad) mostly. Jade's mum said, "Errrr, Jade, what's that near you?" Jade then stuttered, and I popped my head up with a very mischievous grin on my face. Jade's mum wasn't happy at all, but all was forgotten after breakfast – well, I had hoped.

We also lost our virginities together, which made this very special journey even more meaningful and special to both of us. At this point, we had created a connection which was totally unbreakable, and summer 2002 was ready to hit.

Our First Holiday Together

I remember asking Jade, just two months after we had met, let's go on holiday, which was the summer of 2002, but we came across a stumbling block. As Jade was only 17, she needed consent from her parents which had to be signed and sent into the travel agents for us to make our first holiday happen and also my signature as I was 18. Jade got the letter off her parents, and we were so pleased, jumping in the air with excitement without a care in the world other than being with each other and on the beach.

We decided to go to Mykonos as Greece was very popular in the early 2000s, Mykonos wasn't then, but is now, which is crazy. The weather was so hot and also the euro was sitting around £1 to €1.65 which was amazing. We had £250 spending money between us for the week, so off we went, packed our bags and headed for Greece. We always made a joke about chicken pittas – saying, "You are a chicken pitta," and would just laugh our heads off constantly when on holiday. I always remember Jade pretending to look like a chicken pitta; how do you do that? Anyway, she did, and we just laughed all night long. I remember I had my blue sunglasses on, thinking I was Peter Andre, tensing the muscles for Jade, and she was just sunbathing, loving life, as she tanned so well; them killer legs. I remember we would get up twice in the night and shower due to the heat and no air conditioning, the shower always stays in my mind, for starters, it was a trickler, but most importantly, it cooled us down.

Half the island was gay, so obviously I was getting some looks, and Jade just found this funny. I never forgot the gyros chicken pitta in Greek bread with chips and mint yogurt sauce, they at the time were only 1 euro, and heaven just came to mind every time we had one, which was every day early pm. I always recall a bar we sat in at Mykonos town, which had a small balcony going out to sea where the sunset was just breathtaking. At this moment, I knew Jade was the one and holding onto that was key, but I never told her that at this stage. On this night after we had gone into Mykonos town, I was in the shower and came out to notice Jade was sucking her thumb and said, "What are you doing?" She said, "Oh, I suck my thumb. It's nice, I like it, and makes me feel at comfort and ease. I'm at ease with you, so that's why I'm doing it." She had sucked her thumb all her life, and this completely never changed, and it was a key visual and feeling that always brought me back to never growing old in our relationship.

We knew that after the holiday I was heading to university Sheffield Hallam after achieving my business studies A levels going onto business management and marketing, and this was a concern for both of us. Jade had one more year at college doing arts and textiles, meaning when I would be in year 2 at uni, she would step into her first year. We were pleased, though, as we would graduate together due to my course being a four-year sandwich course. This gave us great hope and also created an even stronger foundation for us moving forward if we made it.

Year 1 at University – Saying Goodbye to Jade

The first day at university came, and I was heading in my mum's car where she had packed all my things up, with me and Jade sat in the back of the car wanting to see me settle in. My first-year digs were at Norfolk Park Student Village where I already had Richard Alcock, my school pal, also moving in, so this helped me and made me feel better, knowing he would help me plug into more students to make friends. I always remember placing my small TV my Nana Guy had given me where the aerial for the TV was – no joke about eight feet high – but was so grateful Nana gave me this. All my things were in my cupboards, and then Jade started to break down and cry and so did my mum, and it was like we were all leaving each other, but it gave me peace of mind as I was only 20 minutes on a train away to head back to Doncaster.

Jade's heart broke that day and so did mine, as all we had built up from Valentine's up to the summertime felt as if it was fading away. Being 18 years old in love, and having to move even further away, just broke us. But I knew this was my journey and Jade would have her own, with also having pure hope, faith and belief that if we were meant to be then we would make it through university and come out smiling and even stronger at the end for each other.

Jade went on to the University of Birmingham the following year, having passed her A levels and ready to start her retail management degree. I was so proud of her as she was starting her own journey through university, and I just felt if we are meant to be, then we are meant to be. Having so much distance between us and also meeting new people, this became difficult, which meant we broke up towards the end of year one at university. But deep down I knew it wasn't over between me and Jade and just had pure hope for the next few years, and I truly felt at some point we would find a way to walk the same path again. I did, however, get to see where Jade's first year's digs were at university, which was a nice visual for me to know she was OK with good people around her.

I had just scraped my own first year by the skin of my teeth at 42% average for the year. Lucky, really, as I didn't even turn up for hardly any lectures and was just having a party in life and meeting new friends and people and getting pissed and smoking weed. Although me and Jade were missing each other most days, I felt I needed to stop texting her and to leave her alone completely, which was hard but knew we would cross paths again, so space was key. Has anyone had that feeling of after year one at university, you go back to your old town, which was Doncaster, and felt you could keep living the good days with your mates just like sixth form? But for many reasons, it just didn't feel the same, mainly because most had moved on through university. So, it certainly felt like a new chapter in my life being single, not getting the buzz from going back out in Doncaster, and from that point, I knew Sheffield was my new home. I remember one night looking out my window to Norfolk Park and the sunset, and I looked up at the stars and said, "Jade, I miss you, until we meet again," listening to the Calling's 'I will go wherever you will go'. It was a full moon I remember, and I just missed Jade, I guess.

I also got a job in a telesales office where I would smash my sales weekly, due to my confidence really and ability to win others over quite quickly. Jade had got a job at Perry Bar and also Karen Millen in the Bullring which she was doing part-time and really helped due to her doing retail management for her degree.

Year 2 University – Year 1 for Jade

It was the spring of 2004, and I was sat on my bed in the attic of the shared house living in 469 Shoreham Street in Sheffield with all my top pals from year one, and also Richard Alcock, my good friend from school/sixth form. The bond we all had and still have is great, but I recall one night sat on my bed looking out the slanted window and my phone buzzed... it was a message from Jade, and it said "Hello Pupy". At that point, my heart fell into my stomach, and I knew she was wanting to contact me or at least was thinking about me. I didn't message back straight away as I was playing it cool and was going out to Kingdom that night with the 469 boys, so I decided to message her back later that night. I remember walking between bars around 10pm ready to go into Kingdom and my phone rang. It was Jade, she was drunk and PRing for some pub – Perry's Bar in Birmingham, I think. Also handing out some leaflets. And someone said, "Hey, Ric, it's your cousin, mate, how the hell are ya?" He then went on to explain, "Guess who I'm with and met doing PRing for a pub? Jadalina!" And my heart sunk.... So strange how it was the same day she had text me saying "Hello Pupy". And then she came on the phone to explain how small the world was, and she's having a great time at university and was going great. My heart sunk a little as I felt jealous, she was with other guys, regardless of what she was doing, but I just felt jealous. I felt Jade knew what she was doing that day, and it felt she was reaching out to me and found strong common ground to do so. So that was that, when I make my mind up on something, I do it. So, first thing I did was contact my cousin to arrange a night out in Birmingham with his pals, creating a very good reason to see Jade out on a night out. *See the opportunity and make things happen* came to mind.

The night came when we went out in Birmingham, and to be honest, all I wanted was to see Jade, and that's exactly what happened, although it was the first time she had seen me since we broke up in first year and it all felt very nerve-racking. I remember seeing her in a bar within the Arcadian, and she dismissed me a little, suppose she was still angry, but I knew deep down she liked the fact I had come all the way to Birmingham just to see her. We didn't really speak, but she got loads of attention from men, and she was happy, I think, I was seeing this deep down. I remember one of my mates saying, "You let a good one go there, Ric," and deep down, I suppose I knew at that point I had. Life has all experiences, good and bad decisions are made all the time, nobody is perfect. But one thing I did know is one day I will make all this right again and piece the jigsaw of me and Jade back together again if a slight chance arose.

A month had passed, and me and Jade were texting again, so I decided to invite her out in Sheffield with a group of her friends, although they went to different bars and clubs than us in Sheffield. They all came back to my shared house and had a party with us. Jade slept with me in my room, but that's all we did – sleep. The main thing is that we were talking and calling each other Pupy and, trust me, this was a massive step forward. Spending time with each other felt like we were both slowly creeping back into each other's lives. I do recall she had a male friend on the scene, too, but this didn't worry me too much as I was confident within myself. We were both doing much better at university, and Jade had started a job at Karen Millen, which was good, and life felt like the outside of the jigsaw had a frame.

I remember the end of year 2 as I was organising my 3rd year, which was a placement year and just couldn't find anything that suited me. I guess I was very picky and was looking for the perfect job for my work experience, but as time has taught me, perfection doesn't exist and never will. It's a strange old word, to be honest. How we think when we are younger to how we see the world as we make mistakes and grow. At this point, me and Jade were talking but not a great deal, and as I was sorting my 3rd-year work experience out, I also was planning on moving back in with my mum, who lived in Bawtry, Doncaster at the time. So, this was quite stressful for me as for some reason I saw this as a step back as I have had my independence since a young age and also having freedom for my first two years at uni, it was hard to accept and adapt to this. The family home in Bentley had been sold, and I had so many great memories there growing up. I may have been putting my stresses a little onto Jade. She was then stepping potentially into year 2 at university and really finding her feet, with new friends at uni and work, so I just felt space and distance is what Jade may need as I didn't want to be dragging her down with my own issues.

Year 2 had ended for me, and let's say my grade was so much better than first year, Jade had also passed with flying colours and was spending time around Birmingham working alongside regular visits back home to see her family. At the same time, I was moving my things back to Doncaster to re-focus and adjust for my third year. I must say this was extremely difficult to do, as my mum was living with her new partner and it was his house. It was so lovely of my mum to think of me and put me up, which I appreciated more than ever, but as time went on during my third year, it got even more difficult. Having 100% my own space at my student house to then feeling quite boxed-in in a spare room of a two-up two-down cottage, but I was grateful.

My Placement Year – Just When I Thought I Had It All Figured Out

The first day came in my third year, and I was working in York as a trainee accountant for Jarvis supporting the FD position, which basically meant working on excel and making coffees. I had to get two buses and two trains per day to then do my 8-hour shift to then head home and sit in my room watching movies, no wonder I know every movie clip now. I was texting Jade also and at this moment knew she was having a great time socialising with friends in the week and meeting new people, where I was finding myself closing even more as a person and really starting to find my third year very difficult. And I fell into a deep depressive state, due to the type of job, travel and also lack of social interaction. As three days passed in the office at York, I quickly learnt that finance wasn't for me. To be honest, the people were mainly boring and lacked drive and charisma, and the best subject I had in terms of chat was: "Guess what I'm having for tea tonight?" Trust me, it drove me insane as I just don't do small talk and never really have to be honest, I liked to talk about wild, crazy shit when I was young. The New Year hit as it was 2005, and I just felt the year got off to a bad start. I found myself smoking a lot daily on my journey to work and also around Bawtry when heading to the shops etc. I just felt like I was falling into a hole and becoming very withdrawn as a person. I guess now, looking back, I may have been a little depressed, or a lot to be honest, or extremely unhappy. I remember going out on a night out in Bawtry at the Crown and coming back in floods of tears to my mum and her partner, and I didn't have the answers why. Now I know my depressive/unhappy state had found a way of getting deep within me, and I was finding it hard to communicate this. The word 'depression' is huge as I look at this word now, I guess I could have been extremely low and very unhappy, some get confused between the two, but either way, I wasn't in a good place.

Malaysia Plans and the Holiday

My mum was planning a holiday to Malaysia to see my Aunty Diana, and my mum's partner's brother and Mrs were going, and mum asked if I wanted to come. The costs of the flights were very cheap, and I had the money to go, which made sense, and maybe this is just what I needed. But something came to me straight away, and at the time, me and Jade were quite distant at this stage, and I just felt, ask Jade and pay for her. So, I told my mum, "Yes, I'm in, but also so is Jade, and I will be paying for her." Mum said, "Well, you need to ask her first." I said, "It's all OK, so count us in."

At this point, my heart was pounding, and I got a true sense of feeling that this could be another step for me and Jade, and the next layer of the jigsaw around the frame could be forming. Also, at this point, I hadn't even asked Jade and thought *Shit, what if she says no and you have paid for her already?* And were not even really close, although we were texting loads. But my gut said, *Do it, jump and see what happens.*

I remember asking to meet Jade and go out for a drink one evening, which we did, and over dinner and WKD Blue, I asked Jade to come to Malaysia with me for three weeks with my mum and family to see my aunty out there, and the tickets were already booked. Her mouth dropped with surprise. I suppose I was hoping she would just say yes, but she did have two to three weeks off university at the time, so she was free, and to be honest, there was no reason to say no other than us getting closer. I explained we would be going as close friends.

Jade came back to me the next day and accepted, my heart felt a little more complete, and this was just what we both needed. At the time, the Malaysian ringgit to the pound was strong, and Malaysia in 2005 was so cheap, so the bulk was just the flights. Life was starting to feel better, and I knew me and Jade were taking steps to become that little bit closer. The evening she had accepted to come to Malaysia, I messaged her and put: "So glad you coming to Malaysia with us, Pupy." She then replied, "Me too, Pupy." And at that point, I knew she still had deep feelings for me. They do say you never forget your first love and the little things that brought you more together and us calling each other Pupy did exactly that. The next day, I went into town and bought my Malaysian ringgit, which was about £1 to 7 ringgit. That was so good, and then we only had two months till our amazing holiday, which I had a great feeling was going to change everything for the better for Jade and me.

The day came, and off we went to Malaysia (KK) flying with Emirates, which was an amazing experience at 21 years old. We felt a little out our depth – free food and drink on the plane – compared to our previous trip, which was Mykonos, scrimping and scraping for euros to pay for dinner, but I wouldn't have changed anything. Jade was enjoying her wine on the plane, and I had a good few beers and some rum and cokes. I had already pretty much watched every single movie on the planet, so just took it in being on the plane, bobbing around and being sat with Jade, flying off to Malaysia felt so heart-warming.

For the first week, me and Jade slept at my aunty's house, which was a huge bungalow. I always recall the multi-coloured bedding, and Jade was always so cosy, sucking her thumb and curling up for her siesta after busy days on the beach and at the seafronts near where all the main hotels were. My mum and her partner were staying at the Shangri La Hotel, and we joined them in the second week for the latter days of the holiday. It was only £26 per night in a 5-star Shangri La Hotel, where the piano player and a singer duetted in the lobby, and we truly felt millionaires.

Before we headed for the swanky hotel, Jade, myself, my mum and aunty flew an internal flight into Kuala Lumpur, which was a new experience for us all. We flew Air Asia, but before we boarded, the ladies had a funny idea, which was actually I think my aunty's idea, or was it Jade's? I'm not sure. But Jade pretended she was pregnant, and she did look it actually, but this was due to her just having a couple of slices of bread in the morning, and then her belly ballooned. It was the funniest moment. We told the air hostess, and they treated us all as vulnerable, and we got to be the first on the plane. A funny moment, never forgotten. When we arrived at the Concorde Hotel, which had the Hard Rock Café attached to it, we checked in and had an evening in the hotel. One evening, we headed to the twin towers in KL where I wanted to get some new shoes, and Jade was always on the lookout for new dresses etc. I always remember Jade stood on the side of the road in her tiny denim shorts and all the cars were beeping at her. I said, "Jade, come over here to me, they may think you're a prostitute," and they did, we couldn't stop laughing. Myself and Jade always had a knack for finding ourselves in beautiful places together and always to a certain degree falling on our feet, I suppose we always thought the same and were big-time dreamers, so being in KL was amazing for both of us.

One morning after breakfast, we went on the underground, heading towards the Chinese markets where Jade and I were just in our element. We always turned up with the least amount of money but as always came away with the most items, me with watches, fake DVDs which made me feel I was ahead of the time back home with movies out on the cinema on DVD. I remember also we both bought the same red Ferrari shirt, which I still have today, but I think Jade threw hers out. I even found myself wearing mine out on nights out at uni, I must have been mad, but I guess people thought I worked for Ferrari so was always a funny moment. We found ourselves then flying back after three amazing days, heading back for Kota Kinabalu where we then checked into an amazing 5-star hotel for the latter part of the holiday.

Most mornings I would go out on a jet ski where the water was so peaceful, and Jade would watch me from our room, which was like on the 30th floor with just a tremendous view of the bay and beach. I did take her out one time, I was going far too fast and she thought she would fall off, but her holding onto me tight felt good anyway. I always remember out on the jet ski one morning, I saw a huge turtle come up for air, which was very rare. Its head was huge, and I just felt this was a great moment to take in, out to sea in a beautiful resort. I also recall going out to sea and entering a very shallow, clear part of the coral and looking back now felt like the *Life of Pi* movie where the coral lit up at night and when he entered the island with meerkats. I guess I felt gratitude at this point, I guess I found some fire in me and had some optimism for my near future. Heading back for the shores and Jade from the jet ski felt perfect.

One evening, we took a drive out to a beautiful bar with lights outside and had a Long Island tea which just took my head off – rocket fuel – and Jade had a margarita cocktail, I remember her wanting to try something different. Our room at the hotel was huge, and the bed was even bigger, me and Jade just grew closer and closer and then at times we started to hold hands, which felt amazing, and I really could feel our energy together.

One day we were relaxing in the room getting ready for another evening out, and Jade was getting ready as I was already waiting for her. She sat on the chair in the room, sucked her thumb and looked into my eyes and nodded her head, this felt like we had come together as one, and also another sign language that stayed with us always. The nod of the head to each other felt like we were saying to each other, "Everything is going to be OK." So, the combination of Jade soothing her thumb and nodding really made me feel so content and happy with a truly amazing woman, and she also squinted sucking her thumb when I nodded back.

One day we had planned to go off to an island quite close to our resort and spend the day there sunbathing and having a BBQ. We arrived, and I remember seeing so many fish, the long ones in particular. We had also found a great spot to sunbathe, and that's where we parked ourselves for most of the day. Jade and I started to go into the water, then we started to get stung all over our bodies, but nothing was around us, my aunty then told us there were invisible jellyfish and to be careful, it was such a funny moment. We then put full wetsuits on to go back into the water just to paddle. My mum was in hysterics and so was my aunty. As we had the wetsuits on, Jade, my mum and I went out to snorkel and decided to go a little out up to the end of the reef. I saw a tiger fish and many other beautiful sea creatures. As we approached the reef, Jade shouted "Shark", and she swam extremely fast back to the shore, my mum couldn't stop laughing, it was only a barracuda and tuna, but the moment was one certainly to remember. When we got back to the resort, belly laughter happened for at least 10 minutes and still does now. It's amazing how moments like this stay with you and enrich your soul. This is living, and these are the moments that matter in life.

Towards the end of the holiday, we went to a beauty spa where we all got our hair cut, but I didn't, I just joined in with Jade and my mum, having always been in touch with my feminine side; I sat there alongside them both but only asked for a shampoo massage. Now, this is the future, I only paid £2, and a Malaysian lady would shampoo my hair with great product then massage my scalp for 20 minutes. Relaxation wasn't the word, heaven was, and Jade and mum couldn't stop laughing at me.

We also had a massage at a lovely spa on the seafront, my aunty had good contacts, so the full body massage was free, she just told us to tip her 7 ringgit – £1 – bloody amazing. It was an hour's massage, and this was just heaven for me and Jade. After this massage, looking out to sea, how I just knew relaxation through spas and massages was always going to be a part of my life going forward. Jade was in her element with her face mask on, and life was truly blissful. Malaysia was a beautiful place to visit and especially in 2005 as this was when it was less built up and I think there were only about three main hotels, which had been built up along the coast. We both felt so much culture, and it was in places untouched commercially, which was just refreshing to see. I'm a big lover of food, and at this time Jade was still very much just living off chicken korma, sweet and sour chicken and just basic foods. Malaysia, I felt, was a breakthrough for Jade as she tried all the Malaysian curries, and various spice dishes and enjoyed them. This was great as I really wanted to put a positive spin on Jade's palate, as I just love any food, especially spicy, and wanted to share my food journey and food experiences with Jade. We forget how important it is to share the basic things with our partners, and this is food, we eat it every day and don't share our food experiences enough with each other or truly sit there in the present round a table and really appreciate it; most just shovel it in.

Food was one thing I always had a good relationship with and appreciated and was always happy when eating. Being on holiday is always a dream on the food front for me, and Jade started to be open-minded as well. I never shared everything at every point with Jade, but at one point on holiday I thought if we have a baby, I would want the baby to grow up and appreciate food having a good relationship with it and also be open to foods all around the world, I think it adds huge value to how you see the world and views and values.

The holiday came to an end, and on our last night it was around 8pm and the sun had gone down, the stars were out, and the sky was so clear. We were having a drink at a bar outside and decided to sit around the pool. My mum's partner at the time decided we all get in the water and jump in randomly, so that's what we did, it felt like we were breaking the pool rules but at the same time felt like a good experience and nobody was around. Jade had her legs around me holding onto my shoulders, and at this point more than ever, I thought we had really come together, and the holiday was worth every penny and every experience with Jade. This is just what we had needed, and it was very spontaneous, so I'm just glad she had agreed to come. I remember saying to Jade on the way back from our holidays that I was going to pull out of my work experience as it was really sending me into a bad place in my head and hoped they would assess my case and pass me. But you had to work up to the end of June to pass the course, and I wanted to end mine in April 2005, ready to head back for my final year at university in September 2005. Jade had lined up a job as an assistant manager at Whistles, which was a step up for her in the retail sector, which she was pleased about and also earning a little more which always helps at uni.

When we were flying back to the UK, I remember Jade's head on my shoulder and really cuddling into me, which she wasn't doing so much on our way to Malaysia and was so pleased she had felt more relaxed around me and again, the inner layer of the jigsaw had just been laid.

The first day I arrived back from holiday, as things always look clearer, I called up Sheffield Hallam to tell them I was going to end my placement year as the role was driving me insane and just prayed they would pass me based on my circumstances. My case was assessed, and they passed me on completion of 9/10 months and said it was OK to leave only if I did this properly with the employer. I was so thrilled as I was worried they would fail me and my whole degree had come crashing down and ended. The next two to three months gave me time to rebuild inside my head and also spend quality time with Jade, not always, but we managed to see each other every week, every other week. I felt we had come such a long way and university had one more year for both of us. I just hoped and always had faith we are destined to be together, and she is my soulmate, I knew Jade was feeling this slightly too or loads. As I was coming to the end of my third year, I felt Jade had helped me more than she ever knew coming to Malaysia, and I ended the year on a high down to Jade being by my side, and both of us walking into final year at university with tons of hope for our future.

Steps to Final Year for us both at Uni

Jade was moving out of her apartment and moving into a house for her final year with friends, and I was heading back to the same house, reuniting with the 469 boys after working for a year and then stepping into our final year. Jade's apartment was certainly a step up from the house she was in during second year, and I was so pleased she had stepped up her accommodation and ending her degree with all the girls again. Jade had her job at Whistles/Karen Millen and was ready to smash final year. I never forget the time I stopped over at her student house in third year, Jade lived in the main room downstairs, which was quite a large room, and she told me about the time a black man came into the house and tried to rob them. He walked into Jade's room, and Jade said, "Who are you?" and then she realised someone had broken in. So, she ran outside down the alley without any socks on, where all the rats were around the rubbish, and calling her friends in the house to say a burglar is in the house and call the police. A very scary story but always turned into a humorous story where Jade was involved. No wonder that, in time, she called her Instagram page dollydaydream...

To end this story, Jade turned up for a line-up at the police station as she agreed to go and point at the man who tried to burgle her house. Now it was dark, he was a black man and Jade, to be honest, could have pointed at anyone, she did recognise him, however, and point at him, and I guess he was convicted. Jade sometimes did find herself in crazy situations.

June 2005 onwards, I moved back into my student house where most would move back September time just before term started. Personally, for me, that was my home, and I wanted to move back in when the first day of my lease started for final year. I think it was June-July. I called up a business I knew and started working in telesales over the summer period up to the point when university started again. I moved my close friend Anto in over the three months also as I got him a job at the same business. The house felt empty without all the boys, but me and Anto had a blast, working, going out on evenings and back and forth to

Donny whenever, really, as he had a car, which was handy. I will never forget the moment when we woke up one morning and were heading to work, and Anto went to put his shoe on, and a mouse ran out of it and went up his arm, we ended up catching it in a towel and throwing it outside; shouting to the mouse "go home" was comical. We were late for work, and our boss never bought the story but true story really. Imagine saying to your boss, sorry I'm late had an issue with a mouse etc., they would be like what a load of bollox and that's what she thought. We smashed our sales target anyway, so all was good.

I realised I had put quite a bit of muscle mass on due to so much time on my hands in the summer and was looking quite beefy, and the boys at uni did see this which was good when they came back to the house, but I did feel they saw me change a little. This, I guess, was adapting out of my depressive/unhappy state during third year, or certainly up to the Malaysian holiday, which wasn't easy, but the transition went best as possible.

September 2005 hit fast, and fresher's week just didn't feel quite the same, I suppose things never do as time goes on, you can never relive moments so take it all in at any given moment I say. I had been given an option at university to scrap my 1st and 2nd-year results and gamble for my final year, so it was all pretty much weighted on my performance for my final year, so I thought bollox to it, and gambled on putting all my eggs in one basket for final year. Jade was flying into her final year, holding quite a steady ship in terms of passing. She said she was on for a 2:2 she thought, which was very good. I remember saying to Jade, "God, if I get a 2:2, I would be delighted," as my marks were around 2:2/3rd but scraping most of my grades and what happened in final year counted, this was a huge game-changer for me.

I was spending more time with Jade during my final year and also subconsciously realising the university dream was coming to an end and then stepping out into the big wide world as they say. My university mates were all just top guys, we all had amazing bonds with each other, but being all together was just bliss. Jade also had an amazing group of friends, but I do know at one point most of her friends had not even met me, as she had met so many new pals during university and through other girl group friends etc.

I remember getting the train down more to see Jade at her house. Also, one particular day upstairs in the Bullring in Birmingham shopping mall, I saw Jade still working and serving customers. I remember just stood across the shop looking at Jade feeling so proud of her, and she just as always looked beautiful and took the eyes of every guy who walked past her. This was definitely down to her bronze tan, long gorgeous legs and also rocking body, if I must say.

I remember at Christmas periods we would always buy each other something very small, only worth say £5-£10 as it felt like a challenge to find something thoughtful other than just spending lots of money, which we never had. But the small, thoughtful gifts always had more impact on us more than anything. Jade was always very thoughtful, I recall a story when she was 15/16 when working in the fish and chip shop, she would get her wages and then go and spend most of it on gifts for all her family, Turkish delight, small ornaments, you name it, but this was Jade through and through, always thinking of others, one of the reasons why I loved her.

Going with Your Gut

February/March time came, and I really needed to start getting my head down for university and so was Jade, she would sometimes call me when she needed any help around business, marketing or structure and content around this, which I was always happy to provide; anything really to help Jade. I also found a way of creating my own revision content and also started to put theories and frameworks on the walls in my room in the attic at the university house. As I was a visual person and had a photographic memory and still do, this was the best way to learn. I remember a few of the other uni boys doing the same course as me and wanting to revise together, but my gut was saying do it on your own, and what you get is all down to you. I understand working together can be better, but in this situation, I felt it was time to walk alone and just hibernate/isolate for two months to see what I could achieve for my final year. I remembered I did this for my GSCEs and turned it all around then, and I thought if I can do this once, I can do it again. I remember Jade didn't have many exams as it was mainly reports and coursework, which she was happy about, but I was very stressed as I had six exams all within a two-week period, and just wanted it all over.

I also recall when I started every exam, you had 15 minutes to read the questions and make some notes, but I used this time to draw out all the theories and frameworks that I was going to refer to when tackling most of the questions. I remember a few people looking over at me thinking what's that guy doing, something like out of the movie *A Beautiful Mind* with Russell Crowe came to mind.

Well, the day hit. I had completed all my exams, and all coursework was in, and Jade had completed all her work, which she was so pleased about, and we just both felt a massive weight off our shoulders. All of my uni mates headed back home as this was the norm really, but I didn't really want to go back home, felt like I didn't really have a family home back home, to be honest, so decided to stay in my student house up to the last day of the lease. Peter Taylor, a good friend in the house, stayed there with me, but also his new girlfriend moved in pretty much with us, and we spent a couple of months together up to the end of June.

I recall always sat in the front room of my university house and there were flowers everywhere, and it all started smelling lovely, which was a turnaround for the books from pizza, beer and cannabis. Jane, Pete's girlfriend, was lovely though, and I knew he had met his match, and they were destined for great happiness together. Me and Pete also linked up with some Malaysian students and played football with them, Lee thought I played for Sheff Utd, I wish. I was more of a Bobby Pires, to be honest, but stronger on the pitch. Also, I never will forget the game for Sheffield Hallam me and Pete went for as they needed two players and we both played upfront. Short story is we won 3–2; I scored two, one was a belter, Pete got the other from my assist, and we tore the game to pieces.

The Dream Was Over, a New Chapter Had Started

Time had passed, and I had moved out of 469 Shoreham Street, and the dream was over with the 469 boys, but new chapters were to prevail. Looking back, it was a very special time and part of my journey. University allowed me to be confident in my own thinking and believe in my gut and always remember having the right people around me. I also forgot to mention earlier that on the day of my final exam, I was walking home and heading back towards 469 via Sheffield United FC, and I saw an old colleague I used to work with outside the business centre at the club. I had told her I had just finished my final exam and fancy getting into work asap, having already in my head not going back to Doncaster and sticking around in Sheffield to see what happens, and to hold onto my independence. I remember the woman had gone and got her manager down to interview me although she had told her boss, you just need to employ this guy, trust me. The boss looked at me and sat in the reception, and all she said was, "Are you hungry to make money?" And she did it, passed me a pen and said, "Sell me this pen." Ten seconds later, she stood up and said, "See you Monday." The nine to five basic salary was £12k per annum with a bonus on top. I took what came my way, and it was a one-minute walk down the street to the offices, so I accepted. We all have this idea that once we have a degree, we will get £30–40k basic, well back then (2006), but sometimes the world doesn't work like this. Proven experience is priceless. I thought starting from the bottom was fine with me, but with my degree and being me, I would pass most quickly, and I did just that over a short period of time. It was all about working hard and big bonuses for me, as I knew I was always sales driven.

Back to moving out of 469. I had at this point already lined up to move into a shared house with some Chinese students in the road behind Shoreham Street called Edmund Road, and it was just a case of moving all my things in, so I think my bro came in his car and helped, off the top of my head.

I was settled in my new house with my own space and was working hard full-time earning enough to keep me going and more due to always smashing bonuses. So, I had some form of foundation literally straight after university. Most people go travelling, but I was just keen to start my career early and get my head down and earn some money. I was always brought up to work hard and earn your own money, I guess this was a positive as it made me hungry with shitloads of drive. I always remember going to Netto shopping and pushing the actual trolley home as it wasn't far away, only spending £10 on food for the week and saying to myself, "This is just part of your journey, Ric, life will keep getting better." When I started working, I guess I had this inner feeling which was like tingles all over my body knowing deep down I'm destined for massive things, and I kept hold of this feeling always within my heart when working and doing most things.

They Do Say There's Always a Stronger Woman Behind a Strong Man

The day had come, and it was results day. I was shitting myself, and Jade had already got her result which was a 2:2, which she was really pleased with, and I could hear the sense of relief from her voice when we spoke. I told her I had received my brown envelope and was ready to open it at 2pm, so she said, "I will call you then as you are opening the letter to see what you got."

The call came in, and it was Jade, I had at the time one of the massive 3G silver flip-out phones, but it allowed you to video call, and I think at the time they were first to the market on this. Seeing Jade's face on the other end of the phone was just a delight, and she looked truly stunning as always. Jade had such a unique smile, she always felt conscious of her teeth and mouth due to sucking her thumb all her life, but I just loved it, it was a lovely feature of her face, lovely lips and a beautiful smile. Suppose you know when you know. I suppose the things your partner hates are the thing you love, that's love. Anyway, back to my university result. I opened up the letter and also logged into my SHU account to reveal to Jade I had received a 2:1. I completely broke down with tears rolling down my face, Jade was also crying, and we shared an extremely special moment. She said, "Now you know, Ric, go with your gut and believe in yourself." I had tingles all around my body, and it felt like an extremely important time in life for both of us. I had always lacked confidence in parts of my childhood for various reasons, I guess maybe due to my parents splitting and also hitting puberty. Lots of people were quite jealous of me throughout my childhood, and with my sensitivity, this didn't help, and a select few at school trying to put me down, but at that moment in time, it had all faded away. Jade was by my side, I had overachieved on my degree, and my career in sales had just started. Life was wow at this point. It also took me back for a moment when I was on for failing all my GSCEs, and I got called into the headmaster's office with my dad. In a nutshell, the headmaster saw potential in me and wanted to help and keep my dad informed. I got given a dedicated mentor, and three months later, I passed all my GSCEs, focusing only on one goal – "passing"; not my friends, going out etc., just passing. Why, when we are young, are we so bothered about what our friends think of us? Because it's not like they will be in our lives going forward, maybe a select few. This is food for thought for anyone at school that needs focus, lock yourself away and study is my philosophy, and truly believe you can achieve it, but you have to visualise it too. I also remember writing down my subjects and placing C's next to them. This somehow worked for me, I got one B, nine C's: Boom!

As I ended the call, I wiggled my finger at Jade and said I love you and thank you, Jade wiggled her finger back and said the same, excited to see me the following day. Jade had gone off the call as she said she was going to get the train down for the weekend with me for us to celebrate. Jade just always found a way of being there for you in some shape or form at critical points in your life, I suppose she just had natural people skills and the ability to influence others naturally that everyone just warmed too. No need for Jade to read how to make friends and influence others, she already had this instilled throughout her backbone. So that was that; university was officially over, and the next step was looking forward to graduation day, which was around November 2006.

Jade came around that weekend for us to celebrate our degree results. I remember taking her to Baan Thai in Sheffield, which was a beautiful Thai restaurant, the food was incredible, and when we sat in there, we were just mesmerised by all the wall art and Thai décor. The Thai waitresses were so respectful and provided good service, and it was such a peaceful feeling being in the restaurant. We clanged our Chang glasses together to us and our future together. This was a memory and another priceless moment that stays with me always. We headed back to my shared house room and sat on the bed watching movies while Jade curled up and fell asleep, she always loved a good sleep, and sometimes could sleep for England; if there was a prize, Jade would win, probably asleep on the 1st podium. I remember Jade sat on my sofa in the house and she was sucking her thumb, stroking her nose, and nodding her head at me, while wiggling her finger. Within a split second of all this, I had just had a flashback and all the amazing moments and feelings of our last four years and the rollercoaster we faced, but we were still together. Don't forget the finger wiggle was *I love you*, and Jade nodding just made everything OK, which was like everything was going to be OK, so we had created our own sign language without even realising it, and it felt like our world and nobody else's. It stayed with us always wherever we went, but mostly behind closed doors; some folk may be looking over thinking look at them two doing sign language to each other, not seen that before ha ha ha ha ha ha. As time went on, though, we didn't care.

Jade Decides to Travel the World

My career was taking off very quickly as I was establishing myself and ability to influence others very well. I got a promotion to set my own sales team up, so I was accountable for finding the right salespeople, and also, I trained them up then allowed them to execute my training alongside their own ability. I also led by example at this point as I was still making sales calls alongside managing people and looking after the training and development side of the business as it was non-existent at this point. From the age of 22/23, I was very much wrapped up within my career, and on top of my game, better than most in the business if not number one. And Jade was thinking of stepping into her plans of going travelling, so we were again being pulled in two different directions, as I had made many more friends at my new workplace and was settled quite quickly into a steady, stable managerial position straight after university. I saw online all my friends heading off travelling to the other side of the world for 6–12 month or even longer. In my mind, I just thought that wasn't for me, and didn't want to fall into more debt, and just felt my travelling days will be later in my life, I always said this to Jade.

So, the day came, and Jade had taken the plunge to book her round-the-world ticket and go travelling for six months. I felt we were slipping away from each other, but she said that's what she wanted to do and go with her friends Ro and Tania. She did ask me to come, but I said I was too wrapped up in my career and felt it wasn't my time, and at the time just didn't find it appealing. I suppose this was down to being money-driven as I didn't have any and needed it, and also wanted to build some form of foundation for me and Jade, so something was there regardless. It was hard to accept Jade was going travelling, but I just had to accept it and see it as this is her journey and what she wants and needs. I remember the day came round so quickly, it was the day of me and my brother Jay moving into our apartment together, literally across from the Sheffield United FC ground, so I could see my office windows. Me and my bro were already in a small flat near Norfolk Park, so we had to do 11 car journeys moving all our things out and into our new flat, which was on the third floor, so wasn't that bad, but took bloody ages. I knew in my mind that Jade was getting the train to London to fly to Australia that day, and she was coming down to the new flat around teatime, then me and my bro were going to drop her off at Sheffield station for her to head on her way. I remember seeing Jade at the apartment with a huge rucksack and her hair in pigtails, she was ready to head off, and she looked so beautiful, cute and amazing. I had huge sadness inside of me, but I had my flat move as my distraction, which at the time I was unsure if it was a good thing or bad thing. I waved

Jade off later that day at Sheffield train station to see her head for her six-month trek around the world. I remember our hug and how tight it was and the feeling of our kiss and her lips on mine, but I was also deep down happy for Jade taking the courage to go and travel and follow her dreams.

That was Jade gone for six months, and I went back to my flat and woke up the next morning and thought, *What just happened yesterday? I moved into my new flat, to improve my living arrangements, being closer to my offices, and Jade was heading to Oz.* Two completely different spectrums, but I still knew we had a bond like no other and held onto this. I was so pleased she had the character and passion to travel the world with her friends, starting in Australia, then moving solo west to New Zealand, Fiji, Cambodia, Vietnam, Thailand then home. Six months travelling sounded bliss, but the debt just didn't appeal to me, as I was hearing most of my friends were doing this, a small number have saved up, others have taken out two or three post-graduate loans or overdrafts, which for me personally wasn't my path, but so glad Jade went and travelled the world in all its beauty at such a great age. I personally got an interest-free £5k loan out after my degree to pay off my student overdraft, as it was moving into interest monthly, and used the rest to pay for my bond and furniture and first month's rent and get me off the ground.

I remember she called me from Oz to tell me all about Bondi Beach, and a few other hotspots that she really enjoyed. She then found herself moving west on her own as she originally was going with friends then detoured on her own. I remember her saying she just wanted to go her own way and meet new people etc., which I massively respected. Jade was also telling me over the phone that she was thinking about doing a skydive in New Zealand over an active volcano. I was like, wow wow wow, this girl has no fear. At this time, it was coming to the end of 2008, I believe, and as Jade went on to different locations and countries, we just spoke less and less, which wasn't anyone's fault. But I was so wrapped up in my career and working life, that I guess I allowed this to move all my energy into work, and most times me and Jade spoke over the phone, it just felt like we were very distant, or at least I felt like that. So, the problem in terms of distance and being able to handle it sat with me. I guess I was also just finding it hard, Jade on the other side of the world and gone for six months, and my own insecurities surfaced.

Jade had already been in Australia and done four to six weeks, I believe, there and was ready to trek on to New Zealand. I remember seeing amazing photos of Jade trekking over lakes and frozen glaciers with some friends, and it just looked incredible. One of her biggest achievements was doing her skydive 10,000 feet high in the sky to then plummet over an active volcano. She also created a video, and I always remember she opened up her hands when in the sky, and it said Love you, Mum and Dad. The love Jade had for her family and her mum and dad was just something else, she always told me she just loved the fact that her parents were together from a very young age and still going strong and created this really happy, calm, inner peace, which I suppose created a stability within Jade on how she thought and her faith in love. Hats off to Jade's parents for raising such an amazing human being, who always had the ability to influence others, make people smile, help when times are hard for people to take big steps in their lives and, most importantly, just put people first and cared. When Jade had told me and sent me a photo of her face when she was sky diving, I couldn't believe what I was seeing, but she did it, and I was so proud of her. I remember Fiji and the pictures Jade had taken and it looked just out of this world. But also, I had some sort of association with it as it was in the media around the time due to the first *Love Island* programme with Callum Best and Lee Sharpe in and also Abby Titmuss, who was an old model back in the day. I'm sure most can remember this series. Ha ha ha ha ha. *Love Island* hits the TV for the first time, which was different back then, it wasn't all about being 20 years old and having a trim body and all quite pretentious, it was just ordinary-looking celebs really trying to find love. Looking back, it was the right approach. I guess social media has played a part in the programme change of *Love Island*, which, by the way, was a show Jade just absolutely loved, she was fixated.

The following year had hit, and I kept on getting promoted at work, as I went from sales to a sales team manager, then was given the position to manage all the training and development within the business, as this process and journey was non-existent. This really took lots of my time as I was putting my heart and soul into it, and just aiming for the stars really, as around this time I was so hungry and driven for success and earnings it was unreal. I had established myself well within the business and also had shitloads of confidence. I had also established a strong foundation bonus structure on top of my basic salary, which was a per cent of the business written monthly, which effectively meant I was always guaranteed a bonus every month. If we did £1.2million that month, then I would take my small percentage of that and so on month to month. It was rewarding, and I became a huge part of the business's success and gave me consistency and stability, for sure, within my decisions moving forward.

Jade hits the Far East

Jade at this point was heading for Cambodia, Vietnam and Thailand, where she visited many sacred history landmarks and also got in touch with her Buddhism side. When Jade travelled from Bangkok to Vietnam, she stayed at Hanoi Backpackers Hostel and met many friends where they all gathered and enjoyed an evening straight away together, I suppose that's what travellers did, just came together as everyone is in the same boat. Jade went out that evening and had fried snakes' skins for tea and also snakes' blood, which was mixed with vodka, which all the girls and guys were doing, and it was such an amazing experience for Jade.

Jade settled in well at the hostel and was always taking advantage of the free water, juice and coffee/biscuits in the hostel, anything free she always said she took it for energy, although she would get a full English breakfast for around £1 and was set to plan her Vietnam journey and what to explore. That following evening, Jade went onto visit the Hilton Prison which she said was a horrible experience and then they went onto the Temple of

Literature, ending the evening watching a cobra being killed, which was a little crazy. She finished the night in a bar, drinking with new friends. To completely end the night, Jade got some sort of kebab, but it was actually dog, they had told her after she ate it, but enjoyed it and said it tasted like chicken, she felt very sad for the dog.

It was 4 April 2008, and it was Jades' trip she had booked going to Halong Bay, she had to be ready for 8am, and she hadn't packed her bag – (typical Jade) last-minute Larry. She was feeling a little ropy as she explained, maybe this was due to the dog or the mojitos or both. Jade shared the trip with a girl, so the cost was more efficient, so three days and two nights £35 each, which was for all accommodation, trips and food which is just wow. It took three hours in the bus to Halong where she stopped off at a café and souvenir shop. Jade and her friend were looking at which boat they thought was theirs as they had paid very little for the trip, but their boat was pretty cool with a restaurant area on it and lots of space. The food was quite bland, rice, veg and oranges but she just thought to herself at this point, well maybe I will lose a little weight, so bonus, she was always worried about her belly due to IBS. Jade experienced Halong Bay at its best, although I believe there are 2,900 tiny islands in the area, but Jade headed for the caves, which she just loved and was an amazing experience for her. The room on the boat was to Jade's standard as it had a double bed and also a single, so lots of space for her and her friend where they shared beds, so they both got chance to stretch out on the double bed. The night finished with fireworks and also glow-up jellyfish in the sea, which was just a magical scene for Jade.

Day two had hit, and Jade had eggs, dragon fruit and bread for breakfast and was heading to Catba, one of the islands, and trekked two hours to the top of the viewing point. Jade had no idea they were doing this and had her white dress and jellies on, this is definitely Jade through and through, but she managed to keep the lead and was clearly trying to prove a point. Jade said it was very slippery and steep, but she made it to the top, and everyone couldn't believe she did it in her jellies. Jade really enjoyed her dinner on the island trip, having shrimp rice and veg with the nice bananas she loved. The next stop was Monkey Island, where they kayaked around the island seeing all the monkeys. Jade was keeping her distance and being safe until a Chinese tourist got a piece of wood and threw it, which got the monkeys' attention. Jade said to her friend, "Right let's go", she must have not liked monkeys at this stage. Jade loved the fact that they had moved onto a new boat at this stage and had a huge king size bed and jumped on it straight away, Jade's friend Teresa had the single, so she said. Cat Ba was lit at night like Christmas, she said, and a nice boy bought them a jug of beer and also said he would meet them on the evening for drinks and also karaoke. Jade was so pleased when she got to the bar as they sold mojitos. Well, that was Halong Bay done, and Jade was heading to Hio An, where she went to a temple which looked like something out of the *Kickboxer* film when he's training around all the historic monuments, something personally I've always wanted to see.

Jade was set, and the next destination was Siem Reap, Cambodia.

Jade went to visit Angkor Wat in Cambodia, to the Ta Prohm Temple, which had huge tree-trunk like snakes coming over it. Culture was always going to be a huge journey within Jade's travels, and she just loved exploring and seeing old historic buildings/monuments and always took booklets to read about it at a later date. Jade also went to visit the Elephant Terrace where there were huge trunks coming over the building with about six huge stone elephants keeping up the structure of the monument with their stone trunks, pretty spectacular really. Bayon Temple was another tourist visit Jade saw, and it seemed she had found her Buddha spirit on her travels. I remember Jade always talking to me about Vietnam and Cambodia, and she always said she would want to go back and show me all the amazing things she did, and she knew I would have just loved the look, feel and peace around all the historic monuments. Jade and I always had been deep down spiritual people, so we always loved exploring old buildings or monuments that related to a person or a religion with normally a story. Jade was one of those who couldn't just walk past an information billboard about where she was, she always wanted to understand where and what she was looking at.

Jade's final leg to her trip was heading to Phi Phi islands in Thailand, where the famous Maya Bay is where they filmed the movie *The Beach* with Di Caprio. This movie always inspired both me and Jade, but Jade took action and went on her travels, which was definitely right for her to do. She stopped in a bungalow very close to the beach and went on trips around Phi Phi Don and also Phi Phi Le. Jade was on her way home, heading to Bangkok and flying back to the UK as it was around May time 2008. I remember Jade getting in touch with me so I could pick her up from Doncaster train station. I drove into the station and picked Jade up, at this point I had passed my driving test, and it would be the first time Jade would see me driving, which was a very strange experience for both of us, as we always had the pleasure of being driven everywhere, making good use of the great people around us with cars, but that had ended. I remember seeing Jade at the station and just couldn't believe she was back, she gave me a massive hug and chucked her rucksack into the boot and off we went, heading back to Wragby Wakefield where Jade's family home was. Jade had an amazing tan on her long brown legs and was so thin as always, living on not a great deal and travelling to budget was such an experience for Jade and she just loved it. It was a lovely day at Jade's family house as they all got to see her come back and also find out all about her travels, where she had been and what she had been doing. As I write this right now, going back to this point, I can smell Jade's perfume on her and see her smile. We also watched her video doing her skydive, which was just unreal to see in New Zealand. I left that evening as I wanted to leave Jade with her family. As I got into my car and was heading back to Sheffield, I felt empty, and it felt like we had gone in two different directions.

Take a leap of Faith for the one you Love

A week or two had passed, and Jade was back at her mum and dad's. We had spoken over the phone and also over text, and I had told Jade I felt lost texting her and didn't know if I felt the same for her as I did before she went away. Jade was really upset by this, I guess I felt we were both going in different directions, which was heartbreaking. No relationship is all rainbows and sunshine, and this was a stumbling block I had hit with Jade. At this stage, Jade was back at her folks' house and mainly getting back to reality with being back in the UK and enjoying the summer and sunshine and quite heartbroken, and I was back in Sheffield working with lots of responsibility going on within the business. August had come round quick, and I knew it was Jade's birthday on the 15th and me and Jade had not spoken for a few months. I remember messaging Jade and wishing her happy birthday, but I remember writing "Happy Birthday Pupy" I got a reply late at night and she said, "Thank you, Pupy."

I remember sitting in my room in my apartment, and something came over me, all our special memories, our bond, our cuteness together as a couple and also one thing came to mind "Pupy Love", which I guess was building up over the summer in my mind. It was as though I had turned my back on Jade, and it was like I had forgotten about us and all the reasons why we were always meant to be. She was my soulmate, and I had turned my back on the most important person to me, and it was like I had contact lenses in and couldn't see properly. The following day, I went onto my brother's computer and saw a picture of Jade, sat on a step, sucking her thumb, stroking her nose, and at that point, everything had come back with floods of feelings. I went into my bedroom and broke down for a while but realised I could do something about this or at least try. So at that moment, I said, "Right, bollox to this, I'm going to fight for the girl I want for the rest of my life." So, I jumped in the shower and threw my jeans and jumper on and called for the earliest taxi to drive me to Jade's parents in Wakefield, as at this point, my car was in the garage due to me smashing it up in the B&Q car park. The taxi man charged me £90. I said, "Deal just get me over to Wragby."

As I was on my way in the taxi, I felt so anxious and scared but also a sense of moving forward and dealing with my emotions in the best possible way. I was scared to see Jade's family, to be honest, but was also afraid of Jade's reaction, and how this very random spontaneous action would pan out. I turned up at Jade's house shit scared out my brain, knocked on the door and her parents opened the door and I asked to speak with Jade. I remember her mum calling her as Jade must have been upstairs in her bedroom, I thought her dad would have just landed one straight onto my nose. Well, that's what was going through my mind, but of course this didn't happen, and John wasn't like that, but sometimes you have images in your head, and this was one of them. Jade then came down and got into the taxi, I just said I needed to speak and see you. The taxi man was being very patient so I gave him another £10 to take us into Wakefield town to a bar. I remember being in the back of the car with Jade, and I told her I've been an idiot and I need to tell you exactly how I feel and what's been going on. I told Jade the truth about everything from the point of when she came back from travelling up to the present. Jade responded and said, "Well, you're too late. I am engaged." She had a ring on her engagement finger, my heart had just dropped into my stomach and I felt I'd lost her. At this point, I still carried on telling Jade how I felt and what a prick I had been. We got out the taxi, I paid the man, and as the taxi drove off, Jade just dropped her handbag and leapt onto me, wrapping her legs around me. And I kissed her and said, "I'm back, back for good. I love you, always have, you're my Pupy, and I want to be with you for the rest of my life."

We walked into the bar, and I went and got Jade a lime and lemon and I got a beer, and we ordered some food. I then turned to Jade and said, "Well, based on the outside incident after the taxi had gone, what about the guy you're with?" Although I was thinking it's been three months since we last saw each other, and to meet someone and get engaged was a little crazy. Anyway, Jade turned to me and said, "Well, Ric, it was a joke. I'm not really engaged, just wanted to make you feel the way I did when you left me in May, so I got my payback." And I just thought, well I deserved to be made to feel like that, but more importantly, Jade wasn't engaged to another guy. And there we were sat in a pub and felt like a very exciting chapter ahead of us was ready to prevail. Also, I felt that another layer of the jigsaw had been added and there were only a few pieces left to add in the middle to create the finished picture. I then knew at this point our lives would change for the better, and the only way was up. Have you ever had a point in your life where everything you ever wanted to happen, happened, and you get that sense of pure happiness, content, and sense of belonging? Me and Jade belonged together. Looking back, we had met from the schooldays and got through sixth form, college, university, and also Jade travelling for six months, and here we were still by each other's side through thick and thin, excited about our future together, so in love and the puppies were back. Lots of my friends always say it's amazing how many stumbling blocks myself and Jade got over and hats off to both of us. Yes, there were lots of decisions I made that affected us, but in the end, true love always wins, only if you give in to your true feelings and fight for what you want and believe in. I believe in love and always will, it's the most important thing we can have on this planet we live on. Although I was still doing very well in my career, Jade was about to step into hers, and this was so exciting for both of us, especially Jade.

I remember calling Jade the next day after my random act the day before, which paid off in wonders. I said to Jade, "Why don't you come and live with me in our apartment in Sheffield? You don't need to pay any bills or rent etc., come live here with me for free and get yourself back on your feet, after travelling and university." This was now Jade's time to really establish herself. On the call, she felt a little uneasy, but I said, "Jade, I want us together, period. You're for life, so let's start as we mean to go on." Jade accepted, and she was unsure where to get a job etc., but I just kept on saying it will all fall into place. I don't even think I had even spoken to my brother yet to tell him Jade was moving in, but he was cool about it. I had quite a large room and a decent en-suite, so there was enough space for us both. I think the only deal we established is as Jade was living for free she would just wash up a couple of times a week, but she did do this, so cute with her marigolds on, although the kitchen looked like a tsunami had hit. Jade was smiling again, and we had got to such an exciting part of our lives. I think when you know, you just know, and I say, why wait? Make good decisions quickly, all this means is you get to where you need to be quicker.

Jade Started Her Career

Jade applied for a job at House of Fraser, I think it was a concession, and she got the job which was managing the concession at Meadowhall Shopping Centre. It was a start, as at the time I think Jade was looking for something that was paying a lot more, but I said, "Jade, take it, it's a job, you have a retail management degree, you're one step ahead already and being the person you are, you will fly. Just see where it takes you, I'm right behind you." She always said she was right behind me and always believed in me. I was a big dreamer and always wanted to build an empire for us, so we had a stress-free life, financial freedom etc. Who doesn't want this? But I believed deep down in my heart, we would get there together just because of the people we were, and also together we were an even bigger force.

My family were really happy that me and Jade were back together, although I'm sure some people may have had their reservations, which I understood. But this was a journey I was willing to take. To be honest, the most important thing for me was me and Jade were back where we belonged, together, and our happiness was just about to blossom at a perfect time for us both. I have certainly learnt over time in life not to worry about what others think as this is just unnecessary weight on your shoulders, which is just pointless weight, be happy with who you are. And the one thing me and Jade always focused on was how we both felt, and that's all that mattered. Love conquers all...

Jade had then moved into the flat in Sheffield, I gave her half of my cupboard and some drawers, and she was set to start her new job at Meadowhall. I remember Jade being in the shower and I was lying on the bed, and I had my head on my pillow feeling so grateful we had made it, we cuddled all night, as Jade was starting at Meadowhall the following day. I told Jade I would drop her off at Meadowhall and pick her up every day, and I was happy to do this as my office was on my doorstep, so it worked. I remember saying to Jade, "Let's get your test booked and get you on the road, but small steps." I remember dropping Jade at the main reception at Meadowhall, watching her go up the escalators, and she kept on turning around like five times, waving. I was so in love and happy, and proud of such an incredible woman who had found the strength to have taken me back, and I had the strength to go back and makes things right. I was the luckiest guy, period. We are all very good at letting life take over our feelings, lifestyle and sometimes attitude towards family, friends, partners and their opinions etc., mostly around work commitments, other people in our lives, or financial worry, but we should never forget or turn our back on true love. My motto is: fight for what is right for you and feels right. And at this moment in time, I was the happiest guy alive with a sense of pride, and we had done it, made it to the promised land within ourselves. I was earning quite well at this point so this helped for both me and Jade to do nice things and go places, I don't think Jade saw it yet, but I just knew her career would boom.

Jade started learning to drive, and this turned into quite a funny epic part of our journey in Sheffield. I think she spent £1,500 on lessons ha ha ha ha. And in the end, passed on her ninth time. At this point, I'm sure all the instructors knew Jade very well. She did it though, and got it done, passing on only five or six minors, I think. She was so pleased, but I was more pleased as this meant she could have her own independence and freedom, but she could now drive to work, giving me free time to go to the gym etc., or go into work earlier getting ahead of myself. I remember Jade saying that her favourite car at the time was a Ford Ka as she just really liked the look of them. I knew a guy at a specialist shop near us, so I put some calls in and bought Jade a Ford Ka, I put down a large deposit then paid £90 a month for the car, which was over about two to three years on finance. It was a surprise for Jade, and she had no idea. We woke up one Saturday morning, and I said, "Right, come on, we are going car shopping." We turned up at the car garage, and as we walked in, Jade said, "That silver Ford Ka is nice." I said, "It's yours, Jade, I bought it yesterday for you, we are picking the keys up now." Her smile and face was a picture, and she was so happy. It was a lovely first car, although her driving in time to come was to be questioned at times. Anyway, we took the car away, and she had her dream first car and pure freedom. I told her I would pay the car finance for her for say 12–18 months then she could pick up the latter payments once work picked up for her. I got a massive squeeze and kiss from Jade, and I was glad I could just help her get back on her feet from travelling.

On the Property Ladder

The time came when Jade and I started talking about buying a property together and also my brother was looking for his own place too. We timed it quite well in terms of our rental lease on the apartment etc., but me and Jade ended up buying a repossessed apartment at a ridiculous price thanks to help from Jade's family, which we were so grateful for. We decided to do it up and eventually sell it and make on it, but our heads were in the present, and our offer was accepted. It was on a new estate not in the greatest of areas (Manor Sheffield) but one mile from the city, but it also meant we could have high disposable income to enjoy life, travel, go on holidays etc. I guess we all start somewhere. My brother had also bought a house just five minutes out of town, which worked great for him. It was like the end of an era with my brother as we had lived together for three years and had some amazing times together alongside socialising with all our friends. I appreciate all Jay did for me during university and also living together. He would even go and buy me some food for like 20 quid so I could eat some weeks when I had no money, and I thank him massively for this. I guess you never forget the times when you ask for help, and someone shows up. Jay always did that.

I remember getting the keys and moving into the apartment and it felt like our life was really starting together. Jade got a marker pen, and in the cupboard near the front door, she wrote our names, the date of our first house together, and also to great memories ahead. I still have a photo of this to date. I remember once she wrote it, we kissed and found a new level of happiness. The apartment was pretty battered, to be honest, as I think the guy that owned it had a business that failed, so don't think he was in a good place as it seemed he had put a hammer to most of the walls and also took all the basic kitchen appliances out. We had a full replaster and paint job at the place and also had new carpets laid and also a new sofa was on order. I remember being out for a few drinks one evening and came home to new carpets and sofa, and me and Jade just sat on the sofa and felt like we had won the lottery. Being in love is the most valuable currency in this world for me, as all the small things matter when you're with the right person.

I was doing well at work as was second in command of the business sales office, and Jade's career was just going from strength to strength. A position came up for retail executive of Meadowhall, which would be a major step up for Jade. She went for the interview and got the job straight away. I was so pleased, it meant she was overseeing all the shops and being more involved in the managing of the shopping centre. So, going from a small concession to her new role was just bloody amazing, and I was so happy this was Jade's next step. She also pretty much doubled her salary, which was even better for Jade and our current lifestyle. Jade felt so proud of how far she had come within 12–18 months of coming back from travelling, and I knew this was only the start for her journey within her career.

Jade also when she was 22-23 years old set up a wedding business which she called Jadalina Designs, some photos of her modelling these dresses are at the back of the book but she had the drive strength and resilience to set up Jadalina Designs, so Jade working for someone else, she would only fly, I always knew this deep down and she really started to believe in herself.

This meant we could spend more on the home and we could go on holidays more, which was really important to both of us, Jade already had the travel bug in her and I always loved a beach holiday. We had already at this point pretty much furnished and decorated the whole apartment, but we had one last thing to do, which was to have a new bathroom to install. But unfortunately a leak occurred, which was going into the downstairs bathroom; the lady was away in Spain and came back to her whole ceiling caved in due to the water. This meant we claimed on the insurance and we had a new bathroom fitted, which from a cost point of view worked out amazing.

Around this time, my grandad had passed away maybe a year or two before, and this hit me hard and Jade felt this, but she was there for me in all aspects, supporting me in any way. Jade had this ability to just sit you down and make you feel better within minutes, her presence and choice of words always uplifted you or created a new sense of energy or light. I always felt Jade had a massive impact of positivity on her friends, but this will all be revealed at a later point in the book with running experiences/memories. Going back to Jade always being there, I took a major hit at work due to being screwed over, in a nutshell, by my boss, who always saw me as a threat. The business was sold by the directors, and a new leadership team came in to assess the business etc. The boss quit four weeks later as she knew she was out her depth and lied to the new team about who did what in the business, which meant I didn't get the opportunity to head up the business. All my hard work for the last 4–5 years had all been shattered; totally blood's thicker than water, I suppose. I remember going home and was so upset to Jade about it, and it really hit me hard, she was so comforting and always made me realise and said, "This isn't or may not be your path, Ric," and always found ways to make me accept fate and keep moving forward. But I knew the time would come where I would bounce back, I could see it. To summarise, I carried on with my current role and took redundancy as just had enough and my heart and soul had gone out the business, and I suppose when you don't care any more, it's time to go. On the other hand, Jade was doing amazing in her new role, I remember she invited me to a casino night, which was like a ball evening, everyone dressed up, and it was in the Oasis at Meadowhall. What a night this was, live music, retail awards and a casino evening which I loved. This is where Jade found herself networking quite well and meeting various different clients of Meadowhall. I remember being sat in the Mexican restaurant before the evening started with Jade, she just looked beautiful with her hair down, long legs a beautiful black and white dress with her stilettos on, and always her red lippy on.

A few days after the event, Jade got a call from a client regarding a new position within a retail analytics business, where she would be a retail account manager on the road covering large parts of the UK. If Jade got this job, it would be a huge step up in her career and open doors she could never imagine. So off we went down the M1. It was a Wednesday; I was in between jobs so loved being with Jade on her journey. I drove us down, and we arrived at Milton Keynes where we had a coffee in the shopping mall, where the businesses office were opposite. Jade went for the interview, and I waited in the shopping mall or just wandered around the shops waiting for her. I remember her coming out the building and walking towards me, smiling with so much joy. She said they told me there and then they want me. Jade was ecstatic with so much joy, imagine when you get the feeling of achievement in your career, Jade was feeling all this now, and it was lovely to see; she couldn't stop smiling. They gave her a healthy basic and bonus alongside a company car, which was amazing for Jade. So that was that. She handed in her notice at Meadowhall, which was always going to be the start of her journey but a particularly important one. This also meant she would be based from home, working and travelling to various shopping centres, liaising with top-line management and signing up centres up and down the country. Jade also got the opportunity to go to New York where she signed up most of the shops at Times Square, which was a huge achievement, and spent the rest of the time meeting her cousin and living the dream in NY. She deserved everything that came to her, she mastered the law of attraction without even reading or learning about this.

Meanwhile, in my world, I had found a sales role for a marketing business also based from home, which didn't last for long, to be honest, as the business was in decline and couldn't afford staff. But on a positive note, I got a call from the old bosses who sold the previous business I was part of and set up something else in the same industry but a different business model. The only issue was my old boss and colleague were the managers of the department I was stepping into, but my role was a sales team manager's position. This is what you call swallowing your pride and taking an opportunity and just getting on with things, anyone else would have declined the role due to the circumstances in my previous job, I guess I still had a sour taste from what happened when I was screwed over. I took the position and said to myself, now it's time to really prove yourself. Jade was flying as I knew she would, and I really wanted to get that sense of achievement and value back in my career. I remember my first day in my new job. I had pulled all the staff in, which was around 15 staff, and introduced myself and set the tone really in terms of the person I am and how I want to work with everyone etc. It was a good introduction, and I remember the head of sales looking over at me and saying, "Ric Hart's back." It felt good to be back and with so many familiar faces. My old boss was managing the B2B section, and this again was another issue, but I just swallowed my pride, rose above everything and aimed to prove a point and certainly did.

The Holiday Journey had started

Jade was getting pay rise after pay rise, and she was really establishing herself in her current role and becoming a huge makeup of the business. The summer of 2011 had hit, I believe, and me and Jade went on holiday to Egypt with her sister and partner. We hit Sharm El-Sheik, nobody would holiday there in today's world but what an amazing holiday and place it was. For starters, it's cheap and great value. We had created so many amazing new memories, like snorkelling off the reef, which was just breathtaking, I think we were fishes in our previous life. I felt déjà vu had hit as we were in the water at Sharm El-Sheik and Jade shouted "Shark." All these Germans fled the scene, and also Jade, Jade's sister and fella swam to the metal steps to get out the water and step onto the jetty. As I remember, I got an elbow from Jade's sister as she wanted to get onto the jetty quite sharpish, it was a funny moment; defo dog eat dog world came to mind ha ha ha ha. But this left me in the water, so I decided to stay in the water and see what was coming towards us; it was a giant trevalla fish, it was huge, massive teeth and looked like an old grumpy man. I stayed calm and it swam off, it felt like an amazing life moment, but the whole story was just hilarious starting from Jade shouting shark again. It took me straight back to Malaysia that time when it was in fact tuna and barracuda.

Jade and I loved the all-inclusive Mexican restaurant and especially the enchiladas and also the Mexican burger, this was our favourite place to eat. Jade loved going away with her sister, she always said to me "my sister is my best friend" and she always felt she would always be there for her and look after her in her own way shape or form, I'm sure Sally felt this always. We had all gone black due to the heat, and me and Rob always loved a good shish smoke. I always remember the quad sunrise morning when we all quadded in the desert and went to see all the Bedouins; one guy had such bad teeth; I don't think you could see a speck of white. Ha ha ha ha ha. We also went into the local shops and got dressed in the local white gowns and dressed like the Egyptians. I remember Jade running out the shop dressed like an Egyptian, she looked gorgeous and so glamorous. I also remember me and Jade getting dressed up, and I went out protesting, dressed up with the local clan. To be honest, it was quite dangerous, but that was me and Jade together, very random. This memory was our second Egypt holiday, but this was just us. Our last trip in Sharm was when we all went in a car to a remote part of the coast where we snorkelled in extremely deep water, which looking back was just crazy, but we did it. I remember we had to jump into a very thin stream and then edge out to sea. I remember Jade's sister's partner really needed the toilet and Jade and Jade's sister couldn't stop laughing, but I've been there, and it's the worst feeling especially when you need to have a number two from smashing the meat and curry the night before and have to go with no toilet and bog roll, nightmare, it really is. I learnt this one later in life that will all be revealed. Egypt in all was one to remember, and I remember going back to work, people couldn't even recognise me; I was that black.

I remember coming back from holiday. Jade was sat on the sofa sucking her thumb nodding like a little Pupy, and we were chatting about our future. We said to ourselves at New Year's Eve going forward every year we would create a vision board allowing us to always look at our year goals and work towards them. We were both very visual and always aimed high, and together we were a pretty strong force. Jade started setting goals to achieve in her current role and so was I; we were both aiming for a promotion. Time had passed, and we were both aiming high. And did we both get our promotions? Course we did, and we achieved this within six months of us aiming for this. Jade had been promoted to national sales manager looking after account managers around the UK, as the business had expanded, which again meant a big increase in salary, new company car and a bonus structure that related to overall business activity. Jade couldn't believe it. I remember we sat in a Vietnamese restaurant in Sheffield having an early evening meal out and she couldn't believe how far she had come within 3–4 years of coming back from her six-month world trek. I knew this was going to be the case as I believed in Jade more than ever. I turned to Jade, grabbed her hand and said, "Now you know, Pupy, go with your gut and believe in yourself." Déjà vu struck, just like when Jade was telling me when I got my degree result. Genuinely believing in your partner and them feeling it within, it's the best feeling and can be the most powerful thing for anyone, and I'm sure most can relate to this.

When I started my sales team manager role, as my boss was the daughter of my old boss and the politics that had gone on there, she surely knew I would be pushing for her role, but I just focused on working on myself, smashing sales, and leading and setting an example on the phone and off the phone, and I achieved this. The leadership team and directors had already worked with me in their previous business and knew what I was capable of, and I knew they saw this. In a short form, the business was purchased by an insurer which meant the new boss wanted me in, and that's exactly what happened, I got my promotion and was heading up and stepping into the growth of the department and also managing changes within the business at a pivotal point, growing the team to 50 staff members at one point, when I had promoted three sales members to manage their own teams, and also start a new training and development role working alongside compliance. I had some great times in the business and accomplished a lot, at some great points within the business, and it was a lovely sense of achievement. Jade was flying as always, she had recruited one of her friends into the business and her responsibility had clearly lifted, but she could handle it. We had an amazing quality of life where we had lots of money per month to enjoy our weekends, weeknights, go on nice holidays and weekend breaks away, and any time we had a party or wedding to go to, we would always have a blowout on food and alcohol. When our mortgage was only £190 a month, I suppose we could have unlimited holidays, but this was our choice, we had made choices around lifestyle/quality of life, other than looking at lots of bricks. We aimed to always be in a position where we weren't praying for payday and always skint on the lead up to payday, and this felt amazing. We had got to an amazing place of happiness in our lives and financially really established ourselves.

I never forget the December of 2011 when me and Jade went out for New Year's Eve into Sheffield and our great friends Pete and Jane came up for the night and got a hotel, Ash also came who was one of the boys from my university and also my bro and his pals were out. We all knew how to party, and I remember on the stroke of midnight, I bought some champagne for everyone and we all toasted to the New Year. It's strange how what certain people say to you just sticks, but I always remember Pedro saying to me, "This is your year, mate, go smash it." And 2012 did turn out to be a good year, and at the end on the last day in 2012, everything certainly fell into place. Jade and I always remember having fond memories with Pete and Jane. For example, the time when we went to their first home in Altrincham when we stayed up all night drinking, talking about spirituality, ghosts, religion, life, the meaning. It was absolutely amazing. I'm sure this night will always stay in their minds also as both Jade and I were and are very spiritual. Another funny moment was when we were in Altrincham one weekend as we had a family party at my family's hotel back in the day, and we swung by Tesco. I only wanted to go in and grab some things, so Jade said I will wait in the car, I locked her in as was just habit pressing the button. To then receive a message from Jane/Pete while I was paying for the food, with Jade with her hands on the window like she was trapped; I was pissing myself in the queue, then came out and saw them at the car. Many amazing memories but these stood out.

Steps to Solidifying Our Love

November 2012 hit, and at this point Jade had no idea, but I was in the process of looking for an engagement ring and asking her to marry me. But I was working everything out perfect for our Dublin trip at New Year, as we went for three days and two nights, and it was all booked and paid for. I had to somehow get one of Jade's everyday rings from back at the flat and work out the size, so I knew what I was purchasing. Life wasn't ever about a rush with me and Jade, but I knew it was the right time for us. So off I went window shopping and also searching online for ideas. From the point of when I decided to New Year was only around two months or so, but I was keen to crack on and find the perfect ring for Jade to symbolise our love together. The beginning of December came and I found the perfect ring, so I bought it. I remember it coming in a lovely red box, which I kept safe at home but had to hide it, and Jade I am 1,000% sure didn't find it. Oh, actually no, I gave it to my brother to look after I think, as the flat didn't have much storage and didn't want to leave it in my car. I was so happy to see Jade's face and hoped she would say yes. I personally think she was watching everyone else get married and had it on her mind but thought *I wonder when he will do it*. Only because I remember a wedding we went to at the Ye Olde Bell near Retford, one of Jade's friends, and very tactically, Jade caught the flowers, and everyone was looking at me. This didn't influence me at all, but strange how this happened on the same year as my plans etc.

    Christmas 2012 was coming up, and I thought I had spent so much on Jade's ring, I didn't really have enough for her Christmas gifts, so silly me went and bought her a bag of products from Poundland like shampoo, soap, crème, batteries, everyday things basically, and there must have been like 30 products in the hamper. Jade's face on Christmas day when she opened it up was just disastrous, she acted pleased, but deep down she was fuming in a funny way. I think deep down she thought I was going to propose on Christmas day in front of all her family down on one knee; this just wasn't my style anyway, I'm romantic behind closed doors. Me and Jade were always about the little things, every year at Christmas we gave ourselves a £50 budget to spend on each other, which for starters was more exciting but for us, it wasn't about splashing out £100s on this and that and we loved it. So, for at least two days, Jade was a little pissed off with me, but she came round and we were planning on packing and getting ready for our Dublin trip, Jade was 28 and I was 29 at this stage.

We arrived in Dublin on the 30th December, and I came down with a bloody cold, but this didn't stop us from drinking and going down Temple Street and having a great time. I had kept the ring always on me and was planning on asking Jade to marry me on the stroke of midnight at the point when all the fireworks were going off. I remember being sat in a Wetherspoons having a drink with Jade, shitting myself, getting texts from some of the boys, saying *You ready, son?* etc., you name it. My phone was buzzing so I had to ignore it. We went out to the main strip, it was so busy, and it was even televised I think, but one major blow hit, which was when it was announced that there were issues with fireworks, so they were not going ahead, maybe due to the weather, I guess. I thought *Shit, what now?* So I was sweating a little for at least two hours, and as midnight struck, the bell went off on the stroke of midnight, and I said, "Let's go for a walk." It appeared when I came off the main street on the river – there it was the love bridge – it just appeared out of nowhere and then I knew right at that moment, this was meant to be, and I'm going to ask her on the love bridge. So off we went wandering over to the love bridge, I stopped bang in the middle. I remember Jade looking and saying, "Look at these love locks, such a beautiful, special place." I turned to Jade and said, "There's something I want to ask you. It's very important to me, and so are you. You are my life, always have been and always will be. Will you marry me?" She leapt into my arms, wrapping her legs around me, saying, "Yes, yes, yes!" while she was kissing me. She put her ring on, we turned to our left, and an Italian couple were doing the exact same thing, so we ended up taking a photo together. The ladies were in tears, and me and this Italian dude hugged like we were brothers for two seconds. Jade kept on walking up to people in the town, saying, "We're engaged!" It was lovely to see, and she couldn't wait to get back home and tell people the good news. I always remember an amazing Thai restaurant we went to that night, where we felt so much at home, the same feeling we had at Baan Thai in Sheffield, and Thai was just one of our favourites, it was such an authentic evening. It was time to fly home and tell people the good news and plan for our home engagement do, which Jade was so pleased to look forward to.

2013 engagement Party and planning our dream wedding

We got back home to tell all the family and our close friends and announced it online for the world to know, alongside setting up our engagement party, which was held at Crystal nightclub. It was actually called Hugo's House, me and Jade thought it was Crystal, but Crystal just had the rights for downstairs. How this name stayed with us is unreal, as we didn't even know at the time it was called Hugo's House. Anyway, on we stepped into 2013 doing our mood board for the year and planning our engagement party, my colleague at work was the DJ, and I hired some neat kit for a casino feel from Napoleon's; due to Jade's job she had some contacts, so we got it pretty much free. March 17th came around which was our party date, we had a lovely cake made with an engagement card printed on it. We also agreed to reveal our wedding venue destination alongside plans etc., but I told Jade I would announce this over the microphone to everyone. Talking about the wedding venue, me and Jade never would have got married in the UK, it was something we both didn't want to do. Jade originally posted Croatia, but took it down from Facebook very quickly, as I remember prompting Jade and saying what does our yearly goal/mood board say. She replied "Thailand dream" so I said take Croatia out and let's follow our dreams. So, this is exactly what we did. I announced at the engagement party that the wedding location was Thailand, giving people two full years to save/plan and hopefully share our special day together. I always remember the weather was so bad on the night with like 4ft of snow, but we still had a great turnout. The next day hit, and we had some planning to do, but Jade took charge of most of this, opening her laptop up and also working from home, she had a little more time to keep her eye on things etc., and on evenings we would plan together. We bought so many brochures from the travel agents on Thailand and researched so much. Some asked why Thailand, the answer is Jade loved Phi Phi and wanted to explore other areas which she regretted she didn't do. I loved the Thai feel and food from always eating in Baan Thai in Sheffield, and also many lunchtime visits at Thai Puna with my old friend in Sheffield – those spicy pork ribs for starters, heaven right there, my friend. I guess the country, people and food had a positive influence on me, so it was a new adventure for both of us. We had finally found our destination, as it was between Rocky's at Koh Samui or the Intercontinental, it was a no-brainer, to be honest. We were not bothered that it would have costed double, we just wanted to ensure what we wanted we got. The planning started, as we also aimed to travel for one month around Thailand, having a travelling trip, wedding and honeymoon all rolled into one.

My Big 30th

My 30th was coming up, and I know Jade was cooking up something, but I just wasn't sure what. She had planned for us to go and spend some time with her family at some log cabins near Richmond in North Yorkshire, which sounded lovely. This was end of November-ish as my birthday wasn't till the 28th December, but it was lovely that she had done this. So, the weekend came. On the Friday, we packed our cases as we took the day off and took a drive up towards the log cabins. And I always remember as we arrived, I was unsure where to park, and Jade kept on saying, "Try up there, Pupy, maybe." So, I started driving towards the reception but turned back for some reason as we were looking for the correct log cabin and preferred to park right near there for easy access to our things in the car and unloading. As I was driving up the small road on the cabin site, I saw this number plate. I knew very well it was my good friend Richard Alcock's plate, something like B06 RPF, I'm unsure?? Then as I got closer, it was Alcock, he was with Ashley, his Mrs. As I pulled up alongside him, we wound our windows down, and I said, "Mate, what are you doing here all this way in Richmond on this cabin site?" He replied, "Well, mate, I'm just dropping off some flyers for the growth of my business," and nodded. And as thick as I was then, I just thought he was. Then I said, "Well, good luck, mate," and drove on, saying, "Jade, that's amazing he's expanding like this, but why would he be here…?" Jade said, "Are you stupid? This weekend is not with my family, it's with all your uni mates and partners, and also your brother is coming." It was a total surprise, but seeing Alcock certainly gave it away, silly me. The log cabin was amazing, and even though Jade had gone to all the effort of booking it, we both ended up on the sofa for some reason, but we weren't bothered as long as we were together at night of course. We had marshmallows around a huge indoor camp-style BBQ with warm seats and had drinks and party games back at the cabin. We also had a lovely walk into Richmond town the day after, and again got ready for a massive banquet and party back at the pad and a few more drinks. I remember standing out at the balcony at night on my own thinking this was just amazing, looking out to the lake. I also asked my brother and Ash, my university housemate, to be best men; me and Ash came closer after uni as he stuck around in Sheffield. With all my best pals and brother at the cabin and most importantly my Jade, who had organised this for us all, it was a special time that brought us all together, and Jade was incredibly good at that.

Jade also did a surprise 30th for me at Vodka Revolution, having one part of the bar on my birthday on the 28 December, which was just lovely, she got huge, silver 30-number balloons and I think we even paid for some drinks on arrival, one drink. Jade was always thoughtful like this and loved doing events; if she didn't do her current job, events management was definitely another passion of Jade's. I remember having all my pals there from work and also Ibrar and Ben my old school pals, also my twin brother was there with his two best pals, my sister and bros and dad, Jade's family/friends came and a few others, so around 25 of us, and it was a great evening. We shared so many great evenings out in Sheffield with many friends, and it became a great central point for all to meet and socialise. I couldn't believe I had hit 30, life had gone so quick since the time I went to see Jade in the taxi, and we got back together, but life was truly amazing. We were engaged to be married at our dream destination, we were exactly where we wanted to be in our careers, but life was all about moving forward, improving and learning and doing more and being happy.

The wedding plans had materialised, and we had costed all together and worked out a travel/flight path, which was for just under one month; lucky for us both we carried holidays over from the previous year. To be able to travel to Thailand for a month, get married and finish at our honeymoon suite, it seemed like a dream, but dreams can come true in our world, and that's just how we thought. Jade did most of the hotel picking, but we had mapped the route: Bangkok-Krabi-Phi Phi-Krabi-Koh Samui-Koh Phanghan-Koh Samui-Phuket-Bangkok-home. Every night, we constantly watched videos and looked at brochures, but we couldn't wait to check into the Intercontinental at Koh Samui. Jade also created the most amazing wedding invites that were like passports, with all our plans and destination on, and we also had a simple landing page online with all ideas and route. The wedding invites were just out of this world and a true treasure for people to keep. So, the invites were out, the route and hotels were chosen, it was just a case of squaring the bill which we paid off in full by the end of 2014. But, meanwhile, in August 2014, it was Jade's 30th birthday.

Jades 30ᵗʰ

Jades 30ᵗʰ birthday, she really wanted to go on holiday with her family, she just loved doing things with her family and always was orientated like this, it was something I loved to see. We decided to go to Morocco Marrakesh for 10 nights, I think. Rob, Sally's partner (Jade's sister), found a great hotel 4-star at a great price and good location, Rob was always good at planning a good holiday, hotels etc. The night before the holiday, I was always very organised, packed and all the money passports etc. in my bum bag, and typical Jade, which was so funny to see, just opened up a suitcase, got both hands, opened the cupboard and just lifted dresses into the suitcase and just said, "That will do." I was like, "You are joking, right? Ha ha ha ha ha ha ha." But this was Jade and why I loved her so much, spontaneous, random, didn't care and last-minute Larry. So off we went, heading for Morocco, looking back we had travelled on holiday to so many destinations, Greece, Turkey, Spain, Malaysia, Egypt and now Morocco, which was a place we always both wanted to go to. I remember arriving at the hotel quite late on in the evening around 8.30pm, and we had a late buffet tea, we just loved a good buffet which we nailed and had an early night. There was also an indoor swimming pool which we both took advantage of, we would have competitions on who could swim underwater the longest, Jade always won from end to end, she was like a fish. The first two days we got settled at the hotel it was boiling, quite a dry heat, but we loved it. We also decided to sign up for a day trip out to the Atlas Mountains and also a day/evening out at the famous Marrakech markets. Markets were just our special place together, as we both loved a good bargain and to haggle, and also Jade just ended up buying anything and everything, again mainly gifts for loved ones.

Anyway, our first day trip was heading for the Atlas Mountains and waterfall, we had got up in the morning had a light breakfast and headed for the minibus. Our first pit stop was at a lovely café/bar with blue and white floral tiling which Jade loved, she said I wish we had pottery like this at home, well in time, guess what, we did, had pottery like this around the home. We all sat down over a small balcony on a sharp bend out in the mountains, but still quite low ground, and had a Coke and Fanta Lemon. I always remember next door were selling wooden furniture and large rugs for the home, Jade always loved culture and bringing this into the home, but the only issue was delivery/logistics etc. The next pit stop was an oil farm where they made alcohol-free fragrances, real brand fragrances, and they smelt amazing; we didn't buy any, but we decided to get some from the market which may be cheaper. I recall Jade walking around the gardens, and I loved one thing, which was sometimes to watch Jade just being her, walking, exploring, it was such a beauty to see. I guess that's true love, I would look at her and just think, *Oh, Jade, I just love you so much, you're my Pupy.*

Our third pit stop was at a restaurant which had lots of culture inside and was lovely to see with lots of crockery, and the cooking pots, which were quite large, and also the tiling and wall art was something to see, very colourful. We had lamb tagine and some other Moroccan dishes and just put them all in the middle of the table for us all to share. Jade just loved a good feast, and I just loved that she found this passion for food, as I had. It was definitely a change from what she was like when just eating lasagne and sweet and sour chicken/korma, that's it. Ha ha ha ha. Just lovely to see. Although she took it easy on the bread, as she did look pregnant, but I loved touching her belly. Well, I just loved everything about Jade. Night-time was heaven for us as we would just curl up like puppies and Jade would fall asleep within seconds when by my side. Anyway, back to the book. We had eaten and were heading for the heart of the mountains and waterfalls. I'm sure Jade had her jellies on for this but anyway it was a real trek up and down steep parts of the mountains. I remember also we had to go up the steepest part of the mountain, and there was a ladder, and we needed to rely on a hand up from one of the local guys, which seemed pretty scary, but we did it, with some very funny moments. Well, one thing, it was like a full-body workout times 10, and I don't think any of us were in any real shape then, so it was even harder. It was one hell of an experience to remember but felt good when we were on our way back to the hotel. Before we headed back to the hotel, we had one more pit stop which was seeing how the locals lived, and we could also see people building their own homes on and off the river, it was crazy. We went into this house where a local family lived but also had a local shop inside their home. Jade said to me we must buy something, so we did, a Marrakesh fridge magnet, which to date is still attached to our oven, which is an image of the markets at night. I guess we drove away having a sense of appreciation deep down, we are so good at getting engrossed into our lives and coming to a place like this just made you feel how lucky you were.

The following day we headed to the famous markets. On arrival, I remember the place just seemed huge, but we were in no rush to get round, the first thing Jade saw was the monkey in the cage and also the cobra snakes. She said to me it brings back memories when she was travelling and watching the snake shows and also seeing them killed, which wasn't pleasant. We shopped till we dropped and always worried if it could fit it in our cases. Jade bought a new leather bag, a purse, some oil ornaments and also some relaxing trousers, loungers like Aladdin trousers. I also bought an Arsenal top and a few other things and some oil fragrances and leather bag. The only issue with being out of the hotel was you couldn't buy alcohol anywhere due to it being a Muslim country. I remember a young boy around 12 years old saying he could take us to a bar where there was alcohol as I'm sure most were gagging for a drink and clearly, we all looked like Brits. So off we went following this boy in single file through crowds of people, what was about to happen would stay with us all in terms of laughter, and I'm laughing my head off even writing this right now. We carried on walking and striding quite quickly, just following this little boy. Jade's sister Sally and Rob were at the front, I was in the middle and Julie and John, Jade's parents, were behind us. I remember John getting quite mad as we had walked for some time and if anyone really wanted a drink it was him, and I'm sure he thought this boy was taking us down an alley for us then to get robbed, but on we went still striding fast, following this boy, all hoping we found a bar. I recall looking back, and John stopped, throwing his arms up in the air and having a true rant about us following this boy and the bad feeling he had around this; it was one of them moments that will always stay with us all as even now I can't stop laughing. The boy turned to Jade and said, "He's a strong man," meaning John. We all came to a halt and decided to leave the boy and head for a bar with a balcony above the market, where we enjoyed a non-alcoholic drink, I think it was Fanta again. Ha ha ha ha ha. We all couldn't stop laughing about John's tantrum and also how this boy called John a strong man. Jade had mastered the impression and she kept on doing it, it was hilarious, I can see her right now doing it with the facial expression. It became a classic memory that will never leave any of us, all we wanted was a bloody drink, not for John to have a heart attack, I can still see his arms going up into the air. Funniest moment ever. It was lovely to be away for Jade's 30th, and even more amazing heading back home, finishing off and paying for our dream wedding to come. It was the first time when me and Jade were away in Morocco and spoke about selling our place and moving on, but we decided to park this idea and discuss when we got home.

Finalising the Wedding

We had arrived home from our holiday with so many new memories and lots of new gifts, also Jade had bought little quirky gifts even for Christmas gifts for people. She was so good at this, as when we got to November, Christmas shopping was pretty much done as she had built up the gifts over the year and just stored them, and what better gift to have than from a famous market in Marrakesh. September/October 2014 came round so quick as I recall this is when we paid off the wedding pretty much and also the flights and hotel for our trip across Thailand. I can't express the excitement we both had daily on evenings about being in Thailand. We also had back pretty much all our invites, and we worked out about 50 friends and family accepted and were planning their own trip to Thailand and fitting this around our wedding. We were so blessed to have such amazing friends and family around us.

When we came back from holiday, we just took the jump and put our house on the market with WH Brown, we had a few visits but no major interest for a while. We had one viewing, and it was a young lass and her mother who came to view the house. Jade was getting a little anxious as she felt we wouldn't sell it due to the area and it being an apartment, but I had faith it would sell, and as we bought it repossessed, there was only one winner – us. I remember the day they came around; we had a new bathroom fitted, new carpets and the place looked great for a first-time buyer. The young woman asked me what I did for a living, and I felt this is what broke the ice and made this happen. I told her my name and position in Sheffield and who I worked for, she also was in the insurance industry and knew who I was. I didn't know her but, hey, we had common ground. She said, "And you live here?" I had quite a high-profile role in the insurance sales industry in Sheffield, so she probably thought *What are you living here for?* in a nutshell. I told her the area is fine, even though there was stigma, one mile from the city and its quiet enough. The Manor was at one point one of the roughest places in the UK. Some said to me, "Are you mad, Ric, buying there?" But, no, I wasn't mad. It was a good balance between making money and having high disposable income and a good lifestyle still. Life is for living right? Jade played a crucial part with the viewing as she made a cracking cup of tea for them and it didn't turn out like boiling water, and even got my chocolate biscuits out; I'm sure they had two each. Ha ha ha ha. They walked away from our place with a smile on their faces, and I could tell from her mum's body language she approved. A week later, they put an offer in, I renegotiated, and we agreed a sale. Seeing the sold sign outside made Jade so happy she was ecstatic to find our next home, but the key question was, were we going to stay in Sheffield? To be honest, it was a no-brainer, we wanted to move away from the city as we have had 12–13 years for me and 5 years-ish for Jade. We had one dream; we even, I think, printed out a copy of like a country barn house on one of our vision boards. We wanted a big change from Sheffield but needed to rethink about where. Jade worked from home anyway, so this didn't matter as long as the new location had good access to A1 and M1. I said to Jade, I would travel 30–40 minutes to and from work in Sheffield. So off we went looking for our new home, we had also chosen two areas, one closer to where Jade grew up, or out towards Bawtry, Doncaster, as there were so many amazing small country villages around there at good value. We went to view a house in Wentbridge, but didn't feel it was big enough, we also went to see some houses even Rotherham away, we weren't snobby but felt Rotherham wasn't for us – no offence, you Rotherham lot. We also saw an old church house in Mattersey, Doncaster, which isn't really like Doncaster as its way out in the country. We went to see the house and it was a good price. I thought, *Where's the catch?* But I thought time will tell. We both loved it personally, so we decided to put an offer in, and it was accepted. We were so excited to be moving potentially out of Sheffield and to a new location, fresh start with a change in lifestyle, which I was so happy about, as I so wanted to get out of Sheffield. Bad habits needed kicking to the bin, re drinking too much weekly after work and on weekends etc. Jade organised, and we paid for a full structural survey on the property to then find out it needed 30k worth of work minimum due to holes in the roof, rot, guttering; the house was a mess, now we knew why it was the price it was, so we pulled out. Gutted. At this point, we were close to our Thailand dream, the apartment in Sheffield was being sold and ready to exchange on our return from Thailand, and we had no house. Jade was actually quite calm about this, and I was the stressful one at the time, but we both said to each other: What's the worst-case scenario? Move back in with parents. We were OK with this, but unsure if they would be – ha ha ha ha ha ha ha. But they were incredibly supportive, my dad/Liz and Jade's parents.

The Thailand Dream

It was early 2015. The year of marriage, travel, happiness, and finding our next new home, what an adventure, a massive step forward in our lives and an extremely exciting one. I remember we went to CCC outdoors and found some amazing red and black backpacks for our month's trek to Thailand. Jade's wedding dress and also my outfit we gave to family to keep tidy in their suitcases, this was a massive help. We certainly didn't want rolled up attire for our wedding. I had a few loose ends to set up at work, my leadership and training team were all set to keep the business going strong in my absence. Our flight out was 18 March, and the return date was 12 April.

The day came, and we were all set and packed, the wedding was all set and waiting for us, we had also saved up thousands, so we had enough to pay for the whole travel for the month without worrying, and also the wedding needed paying for, and we wanted to make sure we had a cushion on our return. I can't explain our faces, but when we looked at each other when leaving the apartment in Sheffield, the sense of love, comfort, sense of achievement and excitement were all bundled into one, what a feeling. Feelings are priceless, we forget the domino effect feelings have on our lives and the way we felt life was set to be pretty much up to the perfect radar, marriage a new home all in one year.

It was lovely as my dad and his partner Liz and Jade's parents flew out with us to Bangkok and checked into the Banyan Tree hotel, which was very corporate but a top 5-star. I remember my dad didn't get his bag back on the other side in Bangkok, but luckily, they located it and sent it to the hotel around 8–9pm, which made him happy, nothing worse. We had access to the exclusive area for free food and drink which was around 3–5pm and the infinity pool out to the city was lovely, they even did free sports massages to anyone around the pool, now that's service. I remember anyway turning up at the hotel reception to be given some beautiful flowers on arrival, as they knew we were getting married, the smell of the flowers still stays with me always. We were so tired it was unbelievable, but a guy was waiting at reception to take us to the embassy as we needed to complete our forms for official wedding acceptance and confirmation. What me and Jade were doing was totally out of anyone's comfort zone, but it was an adventure, and we were both together, so nothing else mattered. (Let the rest take care of itself was Jade's and my motto.) I remember taking a ticket and sitting down at the embassy, we were like 30th in the queue, but tried to remain patient, Jade was so tired. We then headed back to the hotel where it was like £2 for a 15-minute taxi drive in Bangkok, so cheap, checked in to our room had a couple of hours sleep and headed for the pool area for the day. I remember some more of Jade's family also came, her uncle and aunty, where we all went on a full day's road trip that Jade had organised from back in Sheffield, pretty incredible really, but she was amazing at this. The following day hit, and we headed for the breakfast buffet, and what an experience this was. Jade's parents were taking advantage of the champagne on tap, and I think me and Jade even had a taste of everything from breakfast tradition, to Japanese, Thai, what a feast; although there is nothing worse than eating loads then sitting in a car for hours needing a number two. The day trip was one to remember, the tour guy had an addictive personality and was so funny, everything he said he sang, and he had only one long grey hair hanging from his chin, very bizarre. We ended up going to the floating markets, which was incredible, something out of the Bond movie when he's going through the market on his longtail. Jade bought some beautiful table presents and also some gifts for her bridesmaids, which was lovely as always. We also visited a tiger sanctuary, the River Kwai and a museum, that's all I can remember, but it set the tone straight away for the holiday and I'm glad we did this with Jade's family. I remember on the evening, we went and had some street food with my dad/Liz near a good location in Bangkok not too far away from the hotel, as he was getting fitted out for his suit for the wedding, we loved how family were being so spontaneous on this journey also. Jade and I were mindful of spending quality time with family members equally as this was important to both of us, although sometimes Jade worried about lots too much, I was always there to calm her and let the holiday just roll, and we will get time with everyone maybe not as perfect as we would want, but they are also planning their own trips, so we just left people to it, which was the best way. It was also amazing to see family and friends were planning two-week trips and doing lots themselves, so the memory bank was bursting. We then said goodbye to Bangkok and the Banyan Tree and were heading for Krabi with Jade's parents as they wanted to follow our journey and Jade was so happy about that. I remember getting to the smaller airport at Bangkok for domestic flights, and we arrived at the plane, it was tiny and had two very small propellers on and only took about 30 people max, but what an experience it was; as we took off, it felt like a paper plane and your stomach really went. It was an amazing experience, and I remember approaching Krabi on the west side of Thailand; the islands and the water were a visual I will never forget; we were entering paradise, and we couldn't wait.

That's one good thing about Thailand, it offers everything. I suppose the ladyboys haven't helped with the PR and brand of Thailand in the past, but what a place to visit. We had landed in Krabi and headed for the taxi to take us to the pier as we were heading to a beautiful hotel on Railay Beach stopping at Railay Bay Beach and Spa Hotel. I remember me throwing our rucksacks on the front of the longtail boat, which was a first experience for me. Jade was holding my hand, sat next to me on the boat, and I remember coming around the bend on the boat approaching Railay Beach resort. We had jumped into the water off the boat and carried our bags onto the beach, waiting for John and Julie; Jade stood there, leapt up into the air and said, "We made it." Another amazing image that never leaves me. I was never really into trekking, but the feeling of the start of our holiday, Jade by my side and having a backpack on all fit into place and felt a sense of belonging. When we checked into our bungalow room, I remember talking to Jade about her 6-month travelling trip, she told me, "Wait till Phi Phi, Pupy," which was our next pit stop. She was so happy we could share a part of Thailand where she had been, and felt me there completed everything, but allowed me to potentially see and understand her travels more and feelings. I remember saying to Jade I could get used to this, as I never really had longer than two weeks off after going straight into work from my final exams at university, but for a split second I felt completely free from the world, the rat race, everything really, just free and with Jade. Amazingness on all levels. We headed for the walking street on the evening, exploring the west and east side of Railay, hanging in wooden bars with hammocks and even got to see a Thai boxing fight on the evening and had a few drinks. Jade's mum and dad decided to stay at Railay Beach for a few more days, but we already had a pre-booked boat taking us to Phi Phi islands which took about two hours via boat. The following morning, I woke up and went for a run with Rocky and Man of Steel music blaring out of my headphones, just loved Hans Zimmer and his music and some other RNB tunes, Hans Zimmer did all the movie-themed songs, and it was close to classical music but wasn't if you get me. That morning, I felt a sense of achievement and felt free and excited for the next few weeks ahead. Jade's folks waved us off, and off we went onto Phi Phi, this is where they shot *The Beach* the film; it was always misleading as on the film the map says Koh Phangan and Koh Samui but its false. It is called Maya Beach and was directly in front of Phi Phi Don. I remember the boat came round the bend of Phi Phi and Jade said that's what I booked for us to stay in and it's the top one, our very own bungalow facing out to sea, we just couldn't wait to dock and get checked in.

I remember arriving at the reception, and they said never walk down to the front, you can if you want, but we just called for the golf buggies to pick us up as Jade did sometimes have a bad back with her scoliosis. The first thing we did was drop our bags and head for the seafront, where we had red and green Thai curry and satay chicken with peanut sauce, it was incredible looking out to Maya Beach the view was OMFG. I always remember an amazing photo I took of Jade stood in between the longtail boats with Maya Beach right behind her. That evening we ordered room service and sat on the balcony looking out to Maya Bay and said, "Let's do it tomorrow, hire a boat, and we can fire over midday." I couldn't wait. That evening we went into Phi Phi had a Thai massage as always, I think Jade had one every day at least, but why not? I say. We also found an amazing bar called Rock Bar and also there was a Thai boxing bar which was amazing. The following day, we headed for Maya Beach, the water was so choppy it was a good job we didn't get smashed the night before.

We went early so we could beat all the Chinese people flooding the bay. On arrival, as the longtail crept up around the bend, there it was, the beach right in front of our eyes. *The Beach* film was always one of our favourites and maybe inspired us deep down to push on for Thailand alongside other influences. We arrived on the bay and walked all the way around, and it was just us, it was a moment I will never forget, holding Jade in my arms, pinching each other as we couldn't believe where we were together. Then one and a half hours had passed, and then all the longtails came, and the Chinese people completely flooded the bay. It was certainly time to go, but we had a good two hours which we paid for. The great part of the day/evening was my bro Jay and his Mrs, Christy, had arrived on Phi Phi island, so we met them for Thai food on the evening and ended up getting smashed at some rave on the beach. I even had laughing gas, which was some experience. The bad news was my bro was heading to Maya Beach the following day where he was sick on the way, I remember an image sent to me with Jay on the beach, done in from the trip. But it's all an experience, I guess.

Our final day had come, and it would be one we would never forget ever. We checked out at 11am on our last morning, reflecting on what was a truly breathtaking view and created some pretty right up there moments alongside seeing my twin bro. We had left all our heavy luggage back at Krabi with Jade's parents and only took a small bag we bought from Morocco actually and threw a few things in there as it was on my back, Jade was bag-free which she just loved. After checking out, Jade had heard there was a pretty beach on the other side of where our resort was, so off we headed through a track and low jungle in Phi Phi islands. It only took about 10 minutes to get to the other side as where we were staying was like on the tip of the island if you get me. The beach was dead, nobody was there other than me and Jade and some funny looking small crabs that ran all over the sand, was pretty crazy to see but was paradise. We saw in the distance two people near a shipwrecked longtail boat just off the shores, so we wandered towards them, introducing ourselves. They were from Holland, he also mentioned that there were some amazing spots further across the island and invited us to take a wander, so we did across the high rocks. After a short while, the couple had disappeared, and me and Jade were wondering where they were as we walked across the high broken rock above the seabed and shore. I kept on asking Jade where we were, she replied, "Keep going, Pupy," so we did.

We then found ourselves in a position where the tide was coming for us, and I had a small bag on my shoulder, and the water was washing up quick, meaning it would take us out to sea. I was shitting myself and so was Jade although she was a little calmer than me. We then had to scramble using our hands and arms up onto the cliffside and move up into the jungle, finding ourselves stranded deep in a Thai jungle with a tiny sense of direction. We walked for about 40 minutes and arrived at this like village-type place. We had to get to the pier for 3pm, and it was like 12.30pm, we had literally a quarter of a litre of water, it was about 40 degrees, and the humidity was like 90. I felt we had stepped into a survival show. When we arrived at the village, it was empty. Jade was walking around shouting hello, we found some shade to get our breath back and recharge our energy. I was saying to Jade, "This is bad, we are burning, no sun cream, stuck in a jungle, no water and where are the humans?" Lol, she laughed and said we will be fine. We kept on walking, and you could see us both lagging, and the sun was really slowing us down. After like 1.5 hours we then saw a sign, which was a massive breakthrough, it said Viewpoint. As we approached the sign a few minutes later, we just stumbled out the jungle onto a road where I thanked god so much, at that point, that me and Jade were going to be OK, it was that scary. I found the nearest shop, walked in, got two bottles of lemon fizzy Fanta and was that thirsty, nailed both bottles without coming up for air. I should have drunk water but just grabbed what we could. Jade did the same then we paid after; the Thai man who had the shop must have thought *hey you pay before you try*. The saying is, I think, *you like you buy*. Ha ha ha ha ha. Most importantly, we were alive and still had legs to get to the wedding. We entered the main drag on Phi Phi to head for our boat, which we just made 15 minutes before it left. We looked at each other and said, "WTF just happened? Anyway, back to Krabi to see your parents," as our hearts were pounding. (Never a dull moment!)

We headed back to Krabi to tell the tale to Jade's folks then checked in for two nights as a wind-down really from the last few days at Railay Princess Resort to then trace our footsteps back to Krabi airport and head for Koh Samui our wedding destination.

Koh Samui the Wedding Destination

The plane came into Koh Samui airport and as we stepped inside it was like an exclusive luxury area for first-class guests, it had huge character and was really quirky. Jade just loved that it had this feel about it, I remember her just smiling with her thumb in her mouth, that smile, the one everyone knows when she has her thumb in. We checked into a sea view bungalow at Lazy Days, where we had friends waiting for us on arrival, which was amazing. The bungalows were so quirky and vintage, and very cosy inside, it was lovely to wake up and just see the sea and the noise of Koh Samui. Two days into Koh Samui, pretty much everyone had arrived at their hotels on the island and was lovely to share all our trips and memories we had created so far. Me and Jade were amazed at the story my dad and brother Andy told us, that they were both in the water near Phi Phi islands and Andy and Tracy were in the water on their boat and Dad flew by on a speedboat. As my dad would say, you just can't buy this, what a memory. The first part of Koh Samui was great as it was really with our friends and going into Lamai and Chaweng eating out and drinking. We had a good few nights in the bungalow at Lazy Days, where I remember getting a car and driving up to see my mum and her resort as she was on the south of the island near the wedding venue. I remember also loving driving around Thailand, picking family up and really enjoying the view and freedom, to be honest. Jade also bought some more gifts for the wedding, and we were all set in terms of table gifts and bridesmaids and best men gifts.

Koh Phangan Full Moon Party

Our next pit stop was meeting up at the pier to head via boat over to the full moon party with all our friends together, where also I met Ash from university (one of my best men). We had told everyone that we paid for everyone's accommodation as we had found seven bungalows in line with each other, which allowed me and my friends and brothers and Jade and all her friends to have a roof over their heads for two nights, full moon eve and the full moon night party. Some stuck their nose up, but me and Jade didn't care, we had done something good for all and was ready to party and celebrate together the next step, our wedding. That's what I loved about us, we weren't snobby, we just always got on with things in our lives regardless of the cards dealt, we always said if we are together, that's all that matters. Our first night we got pretty smashed, it was one hell of an experience to be there, we were at the full moon festival, and it was packed. Local Thai folk propping up there stands selling buckets of vodka and various other mixers with their local Red Bull, which was like rocket fuel and also had amphetamine in as we were told. They were so cheap, like £4 for a bucket and you would be smashed after it. I recall at the end of the bungalows was this restaurant where the next morning we all got a huge, long table and had a big breakfast to get the day started. I also bought loads of vests for the best men as additional gifts, Chang t-shirts (classic) bright yellow. I remember Jade was out chilling with the girls and us lads went and hit the jet skis, the water was crystal clear. It was all about the full moon party, and some were hanging out their arses, but round two hit, I remember Jade started at one bar with her friends, and us lads went to watch some Thai boxing, which was a little odd as there were like three-year-olds fighting each other with adults sized gloves; anyway, another experience for the bank. We got really drunk, and I appreciated all who came out to spend it with us. I remember some got the speedboat back to Koh Samui that night, but the rest of us partied on the beach like we were 18 again without a care in the world, other than heading for our wedding destination.

The Intercontinental Koh Samui – We Had Arrived Alive, We Were All Set to Become Mr And Mrs Hart

The only downside to the following day heading for the wedding resort was we had a tad of a hangover, and on the boat back, I don't think anyone said a word to each other as we were hanging out our arse to recharge for the wedding. I remember getting off the boat with Jade, and we then got a taxi heading for the wedding venue. As the taxi took us up a windy, steep hill and brought us to the reception of the Intercontinental, we got out the taxi still hanging a little, I think. I had my full moon party vest still on, and Jade's hair was everywhere, it was like one of the moments from *Pretty Woman* when Julia Roberts walks into the shop, and all the staff look down at her. Anyway, me and Jade took a seat at the reception and took in what was the best view I have ever seen in my life.

Jade just kept on saying wow, with her mouth open smiling and her chin hitting the floor. We had definitely hit the jackpot. We stood up and just wandered towards the balcony facing out to sea, leaning against the glass edge, still hungover a little but a little tear came in both our eyes. I just knew that the wedding was certainly going to be one in a million, and me and Jade had made our dreams come true, and what a feeling this was. Jackpot, baby. We had booked the villa on the seafront, and a swanky executive room. We moved into the room first for two nights then we had the villa for two nights. These villas weren't cheap around £500 per night, but it was a dream, huge tub in the bathroom and right on the seafront. I remember Jade doing a video for her friends when we got into our room for the evening. We had a tour of the hotel and resort that evening, which was amazing to see and the views just breathtaking. The next morning was a big one, we had a meeting with the chap who was going to marry us, Jade said he was like the snake from *Jungle Book*, I think. Ha ha ha ha ha. He walked us through the ceremony, flowers etc. Can you believe, this is when Jade was choosing the flowers for the wedding, talk about having faith in the process, most girls would be tearing their hair out. He also walked us through what we needed to say, we had a choice to say the words or just say, *I will, I do*, we decided to say

I will, I do; didn't want any more delays as the wedding on the beach was 15 minutes max, but I worried it would feel like an hour due to the heat. Anyway, we were set. Jade, as amazing as she is, set up and organised for an amazing singer who came from Oz to sing at our wedding, she is called Bella Marie, she is all over social media, and this helped. I have no idea how Jade did this, but she was impressive. It was so funny when we saw her as I told her I would pay for her travel to and from the hotel, but Jade thought I meant I would pay for her flight from Oz, no chance, it was a funny awkward moment, but I don't mind these situations. It was all cleared up, and we were set, well we thought we were; the photographer we had planned, her grandad had died and had to travel back to Phuket, so we had no photographer a day before the wedding. Jade broke down in tears. I cuddled her and said it will all work out trust me. I pulled some chaps to one side at the hotel, and said, "Right, fellas, can you commission a photographer?" They said, "Not in the time, no way, but we could potentially make a video and get a videographer." They said it may cost a little more, Mr Hart. I wasn't bothered as it was all relative based on the value of the pound to the Thai baht. I just said, "Let's just make this happen, guys." I got a phone call one hour later; we had a videographer. Jade was so relieved; her face was like the whole world had come off her shoulders. And relax... was the saying. It was the night before the wedding, and we had walked across the beach over to a lovely seafront restaurant and had a few drinks. My old pal, who lived in Thailand at the time, flew over thanks to help from my other pal. I think they went on and headed in the town for a piss up, but were looking at me, enticing me. There was no way I was heading out the night before my wedding, I can always be influenced by a few drinks but not this night, no way. I made the right decision and went back with Jade. When we said goodnight to each other, Jade said, "When you wake, I will be gone, don't come and find me or look for me, it's bad luck. Sleep well, Pupy. Love you, and we will be married tomorrow."

Logistically, the Intercontinental was a top location as An Samui was next door which was budget but very nice although it was steep and had some stairs, all in all, a huge tick. Also, the other side of our resort was Sunset Beach resort where other friends and family stayed. It was perfect stepping out onto the beach as we were only a walk away from each other. The morning of our wedding day came. I reached out in the bed, and Jade had gone as she said. I got the bags packed as we had to move that morning into the villa, which wasn't ideal on our wedding day, but it was what it was. I went down and had breakfast with my mum and Jenna, my cousin. My mum said, "Jade is on the other side, having breakfast, don't go over." I didn't turn around, had my breakfast, and headed for our villa for three days two nights. The nerves started kicking in really as I left for breakfast. It was fortunate Jade's family had a villa from the start of check-in, so Jade could go around there and get ready with everyone around her, doing her hair etc. I remember going to the villa and being on my own for around an hour or so sitting outside. My best men were running late, which wasn't great, probably a few too many last night, and my bro was on his way, which was good news. I had told all males to head to my villa around 2pm an hour before the ceremony. The videographer turned up, and I just left him to do his thing across both villas, but myself and Jade were wired up, something like out of a Bond movie, and I felt like 007 for a split second, just missing the Aston Martin. Ha ha ha.

The boys arrived as I was getting ready, Ash my uni pal was one of the best men, they were all ready, and I had a set outfit for all, as they were in crème and white shirts with black braces, and I was in blue with white shirt and black braces. It all went well with the videographer kit as this was a black box behind my belt and a small wire, like I was undercover. I got a box of Chang beers in ice on tap for the guys, as my dad, friends and brothers turned up. We were all set, with the Chang T-shirts hanging up on the walls for the boys. I was so nervous, so I couldn't imagine how nervous Jade was. The time had come. I took a few steps out the villa, and the ceremony looked breathtaking, with around 60 seats. The videographer was set, Bella Marie was also ready to play 'A Thousand Years', everyone was sweating due to the heat and drinking water, and I was on Chang. Everyone started congregating around the wedding seats and area, and I started to walk towards the front, waiting for Jade; I was nervous and excited all at the same time. Jay, my bro, had the ring, and we were ready for Jade's entrance, and what an entrance this was. Her dress was something to be admired and had so much detail, 'A Thousand Years' song started, and I just broke at the front, but my shades covered my eyes, so it wasn't apparent to most. Jade's dad was walking her down the aisle; the pageboys came first, then Jade's bridesmaids, then Jade and her dad. Jade was so overwhelmed walking down the aisle, and once her hands came into mine, everything was amazing, the nerves had settled, and we were ready to get married. We put our wedding rings on – and how have I forgotten about the story of our wedding rings? I will tell the tale at a later point – but our rings were on, and that was that; we were married. We had made our dreams come true. Walking away from the beach, we were applauded and greeted by everyone after the ceremony. The next part was photos on the beach, as after the ceremony we had an elephant come onto the beach, which was amazing. Everyone had photos with us and the elephant, and it was a great feature and respect for the culture and also for the wedding. Everyone made their way via buggies up to the top deck where the open bar was, and reception drinks took place. The guys had beers, and the girls had coconuts and daquiris. Me and Jade did some more fun stuff for the video, then the evening started where we had a sit-down buffet meal, Bella was singing on top of the jacuzzi, which was amazing as the drop view behind her on Thailand was one to never forget. The top table was set up where all the parents, me and Jade, and Jay my best man (twin bro) and also Jade's sister were as well, as they had speeches. What me and Jade had organised and achieved was something amazing. The setup and day flowed well so far, and the sun was ready to set for another big event, our sit-down meal and speeches. My brother Andy on the microphone welcomed us in, he always loved being on the microphone when he was young, so this was defo his part. Ha ha ha ha. The speeches started, and Jade's dad started things off, he was nervous but delivered well, and Jade was very proud of her dad at this point and even had a tear when he told a few tails of Jade when she was younger. Jade's sister then got up and did a great speech, telling the tale of Jade, informing us all of her and Rob's engagement, and talking a little Thai at the start to set the scene. Jay got up and did me proud, he captured everything and really surprised me with his speech, deliverance and structure, he didn't miss anything and even had a projector with images etc. to add value to the story he was telling. So, here's the thing, I didn't prepare anything. Some may say WTF, but I decided I didn't want to prepare anything, why did I need to prepare when I knew what points I wanted to touch on. So as my brother passed me the microphone and he got a huge applause, I thought *Shit, man, what do I say?* So, I went with the flow and just spoke as close as I could from the heart, getting rid of any nerves. They do say, once you're up there, the nerves go, and they did. I told the story of when me and Jade first set our eyes on each other in IKON, our lives together, the way she constantly made me feel, and trust me; it was the best feeling to call Jade my wife. We had done it. Jade always had her heart set on her surname being double-barrelled but taking most out of her surname, well "grave", so she wanted to be called Jade Hazelhart as her family name was Hazelgrave, but I certainly was not changing my name to Ric Hazelhart, I would have sounded like a wrestler/porn star. The speeches were over, the food was exquisite, and music was playing, and we had done it exactly how we wanted it. Jade and I looked at each other from a distance and nodded like puppies, in love, happy together, forever Mr and Mrs Hart.

We had also cut the cake but never saw it again for some reason if anyone has the answers to this one let me know. So, we needed to head back down to the beach where they pushed all the deserts down, and we had our first dance where the videographer captured all, and we partied the night away. My dad also opened up the evening party with a speech, defo the man for it, DJ AL. We also let off lanterns, one got stuck and went into the bushes, last thing we wanted was to set alight a fire. The evening finished with drinks and cigars around the log fire while Bella was singing, and we all sat around the sign: Shoes Here, Vows Here, Love Everywhere. It was a day and night that will stay with all forever. We had organised free drinks for everyone, which was so much easier and allowed everyone to relax a bit more, and we were so glad we did this for everyone. The next morning came, and we had chicken satays at the bottom of our bed, we must have ordered room service for a snack but didn't eat it. We looked at each other as man and wife, Jade got in the hot tub, which was huge and was our bath, and we had a day of relaxation, and everyone just spoke about who was pissed out their head, the day and night and all the amazing moments. I went up to square the wedding bill in full and then came back down for breakfast. Jade said, "Pupy why are you sweating?" I replied, "I've just paid the wedding bill," and laughed, didn't tell her the amount until we got back home as didn't want her thinking about money, and we enjoyed another amazing Intercontinental breakfast. That evening we had our honeymoon 5-course meal on the seafront, table for two, candlelit, and everyone was looking over at us. I kept on saying to Jade, "Why is everyone looking over?" She replied, "I don't know, Pupy, take no notice." We had such a relaxing evening talking about the wedding day highlights, our travelling journey, all we had achieved, and how we felt about each other. Jade and I had this unique Pupy love bond that was unbreakable regardless of circumstances. We had opened a new chapter in our lives, and it already was one hell of a rollercoaster, we were just excited for our lives together. We also stepped out that evening and dropped a love lock into the water at the end of the pier to represent our love together, held it together, kissed and thew the lock in and also the key separately, so totally unbreakable. Everyone started to check out the next morning as so did we as we were heading for our honeymoon villa for three days. We said our goodbyes to everyone at reception and headed for the airport where we were flying to Phuket. What a wedding, what an experience, it's all about the journey, ride it and don't look back.

The Honeymoon – The end of the Thailand Dream

For three whole days at the villa, I think Jade just slept, and when she woke it was time to eat then, she slept again. It was so cute to see, but she must have just been mentally exhausted from the trip and more importantly the lead up to the wedding, so I would relax swim and read my books. The villa was a two-story villa with a cinema room and infinity pool, we also had one of the best Thai massages on the complex it cost a little more, but we didn't care. One evening during Phuket, we went into the town, had some drinks and street food, I bought some watches like a proper Delboy, and we also walked through the main night scene in Phuket. We personally didn't like it, a little too dirty and lots of ladyboys around, this I suppose was the reason why Thailand had been stamped on from a PR perspective over the years, but everything else outweighed this side to Thailand. I remember going into a back shop off the main road to buy my watches. We were mad on how we went about things, but life wasn't really about caution for me and Jade, we liked to live life on the edge together, enjoying ourselves, travelling, spending money.

Bangkok the Final Leg Home Hangover 2 Was Coming to an End.

The Thailand Dream was over, and Jade was getting quite down as we had to travel back home, and back to our empty flat, as Jade had sold all the furniture on Shpock for next to nothing on my stag weekend in Manchester a couple of months before the wedding. I had walked in on the Sunday that weekend and was like, "Jade, where's all our stuff?" She just did her little cute giggle and said, "Sorry, Pupy, I Shpocked it all this weekend, do you like the space?" It was a moment to remember. Before the dream and party ended, we still had Bangkok left to hit, so on arrival, we stored our bags and had a full day in the city and also the evening when we met Jade's friends on Koh San Road, which is quite a cool area, for food, drinks and street food, it's near the big Buddha and famous temples. First, we got some pad Thai with prawns and chicken with Jade's friends Ro and Tania, and I remember us meeting Jade's friends Rachel and Sam also. We all ended up getting on it, eating scorpions and reminiscing over the Thailand trip and best memories.

It was time to say our farewells and head for the airport, half-cut from beer, cocktails and the shots we had. I remember the main desk offering us to give our seats up to some people who wanted them. I think it was something to do with a football match, but we said no, we need to get back home. Little did we bloody realise they were actually offering if they put us up in a hotel for one night and we flew back home the next day. Free flights back to Thailand! Dropped a bollock there but you live and learn, we blamed the shots. The dream had come to an end, we were flying back to one of the roughest estates in England that had no furniture, we certainly were going from hot to cold, but more importantly, we were in love, married and had a new chapter to create in our lives.

When the plane took off, it felt like we were in the air for days, but it was so amazing to go back married, and our rings were amazing, we even had Pupy Love engraved inside both of our rings. As I sat on the plane looking at our rings, it took me back to when we nearly could have had no rings literally. The story goes like this, me and Jade went to a jewellers in Sheffield where he made our ring bespoke to exactly how we wanted, but there was a slight hiccup the day I went and collected the rings. I remember I woke that day, drove down to the jewellers and as I walked into the shop, the shop owner had blood all over him and was a little shook up. The short story is, as he was walking from his car to the shop that had our wedding rings in, he got mugged at knifepoint, and the mugger was running down Ecclesall Road in Sheffield. The police tracked him down and caught him after 20 minutes, thanks to the general public, most importantly, the shopkeeper got his rings back, and most importantly he was OK, and we had our rings for the wedding. Jade's face when I told her this was a picture, how things could have been different as this was days before flying out to Thailand. Everything went to plan, everything was perfect, me and Jade were married, life was precious, and we were lucky to be together.

Back to Reality but so Much to Look Forward To.

The moment we stepped back in our flat, no lie, our bed mattress was on the floor in the front room, with a TV in the corner on no stand, and that's it. Black bin bags of clothes etc. Jade just walked into the front room, dropped her backpack and cried, as she really missed Thailand. I said, "Right, that's that, let's pack everything up, and at the weekend we are moving out." She said, "What are we going to do?" as the flat was ready to exchange, and we hadn't found our home yet. So, we decided to pack up and move in with my dad and Liz at their home in Retford for a short while until we found our house. An extremely kind gesture, but it takes pride pushed to one side to do this, but me and Jade just got on with things. The party wasn't completely over yet, as we had our home do in Sheffield on that Friday for people who couldn't make Thailand, which was quite a lot, we had 100-plus arrive. We had a photographer at this one thanks to Sarah, Jade's friend, who sorted this for us, which was lovely. We actually decided to put our wedding outfits back on, which added a better feel for me and Jade anyway to the party. Jade getting her wedding dress back on was a dream, so she was buzzing again.

We got to relive our first dance, weddings songs, and had a great gathering for everyone to share, the best men had their outfits back on, and the bridesmaids too. Jade was doing the love train with her family and friends, which was an image which always stays with everyone. We had a huge food spread and cake, and it was just amazing for me to spend time with people who couldn't make Thailand. For me personally, I was gutted the rest of the 469 boys and partners couldn't make it, but I understood why by all, just missed them there, I guess, in Thailand, missing jigsaw piece and all that jazz. It was lovely to just bring everyone under one roof for one night only as my dad would say, and as he said when he opened up our evening party in Thailand for the beach party. We even had palm trees and a little paradise feel in one corner where people could have photos, and we captured some beauties, everyone looked fresh as a daisy, due to their tans etc. It's amazing what a tan does to your look and feel. At this point, business was going well for me, my department was smashing it and growing even more, Jade's job role was evolving, and she was taking on more responsibility looking after the business's largest clients.

The weekend hit, we waved goodbye to Sheffield and all the memories created, and it was a great start to our journey together, and on we went to my dad's house. It was very kind of Dad and Liz to let us stay, but we only stayed there for 4–5 weeks as Jade just felt more comfy at her parents and also felt she was in Dad/ Liz's way, guess this is how most women feel. I reassured Jade, chill and don't analyse things and what people may think too much (I guess it's hard living under someone else's roof), but four weeks later we headed for Jade's parents in Wragby, Wakefield; proper gypsies for the summer of 2015. Something amazing happened during our stay at Dad/Liz's, which was that we viewed a house that Jade's sister found on Rightmove in Misterton, Doncaster. It was a 3-bedroom barn conversion in the countryside, the previous owner was the captain of Doncaster Rovers at the time, but I think Brighton bought him and he headed down south, also clearly wanted a sale. When we turned up for the viewing, we both were like wow wow wow wow, the feel of the village was lovely with amazing amenities, the barn was so long, about 110 feet, with a large front garden, outside shed, and huge drive. The house was renovated and specced-out well. As we approached, Jade said, "Can you hear that upstairs?" It was like someone was walking upstairs, a ghost maybe, she said. It didn't scare us anyway. The lady showed us around, the front room was like 43-foot-long and appealed as we loved lots of living space in our main room. three doors down was a pub called the Red Hart, was this a sign?? Jade got back in the car and broke down in tears and just said, "Pupy, I love it, I want it, that's our house." We had to do our best to get it. The next day we got a call from the estate agents that showed us around. She said, "I'm really sorry, but I shouldn't have shown you around as the house had already sold." Why we got the opportunity to look around was very rare and doesn't really happen at all once homes have sold, but we were gutted. It was like someone had taken a massive piece out of our jigsaw, and felt we had just hit rock bottom, Jade was upset, but we had no other choice to bounce back. It was a Sunday, and Jade was with her family somewhere, and I had seen a lovely barn type house, nothing like Swallowsnest but it was for sale in

Mattersey the same village we pulled out on the church home, you can tell we had decided our location to potentially live. I thought, what the hell I'm not waiting around, so I jumped on my road bike and cycled from Retford to Mattersey, knocked on the guy's door, and said, "Hi, mate, I know it's a Sunday, and I've not called the estate agents but fancied looking around your home as I'm interested." He was a nice chap, very ballsy of me but that's me sometimes. I called Jade straight after and said, "Look, it's not Swallowsnest, but it's the next best thing, go view it tomorrow, let me know what you think, and let's maybe put an offer in if you're happy." Jade did go and view it the following day, but what was about to happen was pure fate, inevitability, which me and Jade believed in so much. Moments after Jade visited the house in Mattersey, she called me up and said, "I like it, let's put an offer in, let me call the agents with a price we agreed," and we went from there, exciting times. Ten minutes later, I had a call from Jade. It was like she had won the lottery and had 50 bags of skittles, she said, "Pupy, you never guess what? I was just about to dial the estate agents to put an offer in, and my phone rang, it was WH Brown about Swallowsnest, the buyer had fallen through due to them not being able to get a mortgage for it, so it was ours if we wanted it." I think Jade panicked at this stage, but she went, "Right, what's it on for? This is our offer." They called Jade back in two minutes and told her it was accepted, and all this happened in 5 minutes. Bearing in mind I thought she was calling me back re the offer for the house in Mattersey, but she called with bundles of joy about Swallowsnest. She said, "It's ours, Pupy, it's ours, Swallowsnest is ours. They called me to say it's available, so I put an offer in, and it was accepted." I was like wtf you haven't run this by me, the price what we went in at, she said we got £10k knocked off the asking price. I was like good work, Jade, she did it all herself. That was that; it was ours. Jade was overwhelmed, and I just can't write the excitement she had, but I'm sure many can picture her face right now. There was only one piece missing left in the middle of the jigsaw, and that was creating a family, but one step at a time I thought.

We moved in with Jade's family, I stacked loads of weight on due to working 12-hour days and eating at 9pm every night and going to bed with 1,000 calories in my belly for bed. I can remember when my trousers started bursting out of a 36-inch waist, not a good look, trust me. I think Julie, Jade's mum, was feeding me up too much, but it was lovely, we had tea on the table at night. Jade enjoyed working on the garden at her parent's house and felt like she had come home but with me. I knew she was really happy being back at her parents for the summer and was looking forward to our move-in date in September. I remember going to my sister's hot tub party for the weekend, and after the night out, me and Jade got in the hot tub. Little did I know that there was no cleaning product in the tub, I was having a right good old dip also, like a bath. Monday struck, and I fell so ill my temperature was hitting 40, and I had all these spots coming out of my hair follicles. I was so ill for the whole week, especially when my sister Alanna said on the phone, "Oh shit, Ric, I forgot to put cleaner in the tub." Anyway, I was bed-bound for seven days at least with Jade's mum looking after me, I guess I was losing weight, which was a good thing. When I got better, I went to my doctor in Sheffield, and he told me I got hot tub folliculitis, I couldn't actually believe it was an illness, but in short, all the bacteria had got into my follicles and entered my body. Very dangerous, actually, but I was alive, and I'm sure Jade was happy about that. Ha ha ha ha.

Swallowsnest Our Dream Home

September 2015 came round very quick. I looked like John Candy, Jade was as beautiful as ever, always fresh as a daisy, and we were packed to head for our new home. The easy thing was, we didn't have any furniture really, as Jade sold it all on my stag weekend remember, so we filled the golf and my BMW and off we went leaving a few things in Jade's parent's garage but, no messing really. As we walked into the house and turned the key, Jade said, "Hello, our new amazing home," and we danced in the living room like Joey and Chandler from *Friends* when their pizza had arrived. Sally, Jade's sister, came round and they made us a Thai curry to celebrate our new home. I remember I made up a bed with some outdoor seat cushions for Jade and a blanket and pillow, and she was sat up reading the paper, Jade never read the paper, but anyway we sat down in pure peace and looked at our home as you do, thinking of things to do. But I just can't explain how much excitement we had, and 2015 had been such a journey with the wedding and also the moving out of Sheffield and back and forth from parents' homes to then find ourselves in our dream home. What a journey, but it was worth it, with mixed emotions, but we got there somehow. Belief, I believe, made this happen, inevitability. The home started taking real shape, and to be honest, Jade just wanted to choose everything and make it her own, taking over really. Most would compromise, but I, to be honest, didn't care too much as long as I had my bat cave, which was effectively my office area, and also where I trained on my spinner bike and had a punch-bag. Jade bought the most floral, colourful sofa any guy could imagine with also duck-egg furniture everywhere. Women's magazines started appearing everywhere, that's when I did step in, ha ha ha. But I didn't mind Jade making the place beautiful, as I knew I would be spending most my time in my office and also my own little snug area, which had a separate sofa TV area, but we always found ourselves being by each other's side on evenings anyway. I remember one of my pals coming into the house, who has unfortunately passed away now, but he said, "Bloody hell, Ric, do you live here? It's like the set on *Loose Women*." Ha ha ha ha ha ha.

2015 was coming to an end, Christmas was one to remember. We had bought a 12-foot Christmas tree as the main room could take it, due to the high ceilings, and we had Christmas lights all along the beams. Jade wanted to also host Christmas dinner, having all her family around, so that's what we did. The day was hilarious and full of joy. We had set up a 14-seater table in the front room. The starters came out, and Jade had served everyone and realised there wasn't enough for herself for the prawn cocktail. I think we all gave some to her and carried on with the Christmas dinner; Jade deep down didn't care as long as everyone else was happy. This was Jade through and through. We then had a break from the main course and in between Jade's dad had set fire to the table with one of the candles and napkins, I think. It was quite a high flame, more importantly, our house didn't burn down, and we could commence the main. We ate for England that day and also played and sang songs till late at night. I woke up the next day and said to Jade, "Look at me, Jade. I look like John Candy, only being 5ft 8 inch in height and coming in around 16 stone, beast…" Jade said, "I love you, Ric, you will lose it, I know you, don't worry it's Christmas."

New year's we invited Jade's friends around and had a bit of a *Come Dine With Me* experience where some took the starters, the mains, and deserts etc. It was really refreshing actually, and me and Jade had a sweet shop also for the party. The girls were dressed up as hula girls, and we also had coconuts with alcohol cocktails, it was lovely. I never forget a photo that was taken of me and Jade that evening, Jade was gorgeous, and we had one hell of a year, but it was official: I was a fat twat, and I needed to do something about it, as I knew at this point my health and life could go one way or another. Of course, I chose to train hard into 2016 and take back control of my life and my health/wellbeing. Just imagine if I didn't take this step, I believe right now I would be a walking heart attack waiting to happen.

A New Journey Ahead

The start of 2016 was a strange one, we were building our home up and decorating, alongside having Thailand blues as it was coming up to nearly one year since we flew off for our Thailand dream. It was around February 2016, I remember being sat at my desk at lunchtime, and as always, checking flights for Thailand. I came across some flights for around £330 PP return to Bangkok, which was just bloody amazing. I called Jade straight away and said, "Let's book it, we can work the rest out and where to go etc., but let's secure the return flights." Well, wow, we had booked it and were looking forward to another two weeks back in Thailand. I put my dates in at work, as I was a top boss, I suppose these were the benefits of not having to work around current staff. Jade was so excited to get the backpacks out and start planning a new adventure in Thailand. We sat down at home on evenings that week and planned our trip, Jade was sucking her thumb looking at the YouTube videos when I was trying to talk to her, she would just murmur. She was like a little baby with her dummy in, it was the cutest. I said to Jade, "Just imagine if people saw the way we are with each other. I think they would laugh their heads off." Some knew, anyway, most didn't. So the plan for Thailand was a new one totally, we planned to go to Bangkok, Trang, Pak Bara, Koh Lipe, Koh Ngai, Koh Lanta, Krabi, Bangkok. This was a full trek of the west side of Thailand and turned out to be a trip of a lifetime and topped the wedding, to be honest, in terms of route and where we were. It took about 10 hours to get over to Koh Lipe, which was like a new untouched Phi Phi really. We had to travel to Trang via flight, then taxi to Pak Bara pier, then a speedboat over to Koh Lipe, which took about two hours. Now this island wasn't just another Thai island, it touched our hearts from the word go. The good thing about our trip is we had no hotels or transfers booked, we just rocked up at Bangkok and went from there, booking things on our phones, which we found more exciting. There were no cars on Koh Lipe, just boat and motorbike taxis whizzing around the walking streets. Jade and I stopped in a remote tree bungalow, but we didn't like it, so we moved out and checked in at Sunrise beach, literally on the seafront where we had our own bamboo hut and also an outdoor bathroom, which was so cool, especially having a shower, Jade loved it.

There were so many cool wooden bars with cool seating, huge cushions although the ants would bite. At night, the coral would wash up on the beach, and the shore would glow up, just paradise at all angles. Koh Lipe was beautiful and became our favourite island by far. We also did a full-day boat trip which I will come onto shortly, but before the boat trip, we spent our wedding anniversary at Serendipity resort, where we needed to get a short boat ride to the edge of the island then swim up to the resort, just amazing. We had massaman curry and Thai green and had cocktails to celebrate one year being married, and what a year, looking out to what was one of the best views I've ever seen. Koh Lipe town at night was not too busy but had a really busy friendly feel to it, amazing fish buffets and also an amazing bar situated in the heart of the walking street, where we sat down, drank and listened to live music. 'Over the Rainbow' came on, which made Jade cry due to this being Jade's gran's funeral song that her cousin sang. I remember getting our wedding rings out and deciding to take a photo of them together on this blue and gold cloth, the image was something else, which I still have now on my phone. We also loved Pattaya Beach on Lipe, this was a sunset beach pretty much, but is where all the bars were located, there's something about wooden bars on the beach we just loved. The next day was a day to remember in terms of stories to tell etc. Firstly, me and Jade were sunbathing on the morning around 9am, as our boat trip wasn't till 10am, I remember being sat down near Jade, and running my hands through the sand. I said to Jade, "Look at this rock, it's a strange colour." I then turned my smell senses on to realise it was a piece of shit. I was like wtf, and threw it, bastard dogs. Jade was in hysterics, belly laughter at its climax, and tears running down her face. I remember saying to Jade, "Let's not talk about this again," but what happened on the boat trip topped the lot. We saw so much on the boat trip snorkelling at certain spots, swimming up to shores, monkey beach was eventful, one bit a guy, angry little buggers them things if you taunt them with food, suppose it was his own fault. We also had our lunch on monkey beach, which I thought was a silly idea due to monkeys around you and you just couldn't relax eating your food, but anyway the food was fried egg Thai curry and rice. We were so hungry so ate it all, and then were heading back to Koh Lipe. As the boat started, my stomach went, and when you know you need a number two, you need a number two, it was the most awkward moment ever, but I didn't care, all I thought was *I will never see these people again.* I told the guy to stop the boat, jumped back onto the shore, working out where I was going to go for the toilet. Jade looked a little worried, but anyway, my focus was finding my spot. I saw all the monkeys in the bushes, so that was a no-go, so ran around the beach bend to then pull my pants down and run into the water naked. As I did this, there was a woman sunbathing, I think her mouth hit the ground with what she was seeing, but anyway at this time I was in the water and had no choice to have a number two in the sea. Well, for starters, it was very clean, but the only issue is, shit was all around me, and I couldn't swim away from it. I then came back to shore, put my trunks back on, said "madam" to this lady and walked off feeling like a million dollars and two-pound lighter. As I climbed back on the boat, Jade said "don't say a word", and looked so embarrassed, but hey, these are life experiences, and I got through it. We then the next day set sail on the speed boat for an island called Koh Ngai. Now, this island only had two resorts on, no shops, roads and was a tiny island. We had a bungalow on the beach, and this was like another world, I remember I got a really bad rash on my legs, but it went after two days, and Jade was browning beautifully. This island was also one mile away from the Emerald Caves which Jade raved about and always wanted to do. We decided to get a longtail boat over to the caves one morning, I think a 14-year-old boy drove us over there and also dragged us with a rope into pitch-black caves, which then opened up to on oval of a beach internally within the cave. I couldn't believe where we were or what had just happened, we were either mad or just wanted to live life, a little bit of both, I think. Again, we arrived early so had the beach and cave to ourselves, but it got busy, so we left under an hour-ish. I remember coming out the cave, as the water and tide was coming in, we had to swim underwater with our life jackets on, under a rock, and pop up at the other end, this was freaking scary, but we had no choice and did it. The boy had his torch, and the water was so turquoise. As we got back on the boat, all we thought was we are alive, and that was scary shit, cuddling and holding each other's hand. Koh Lanta and Krabi were our final islands, which were most definitely a wind-down, and then we headed for Bangkok, although we got absolutely smashed the night before flying back home, as we met an English guy with his Thai wife. He was from Birmingham, so Jade got common ground with him straight away, but we all just got on really well. It was at

Sukhumvit 11 where we stayed. The day after we headed into the Thai massage shop where I was getting massaged hungover, with a pair of dog shorts on, which I needed to wear for the massage as mine were denim, I think. We then headed over to Koh San Road for the afternoon to celebrate Song Kran, the Thai New Year, where the tradition for this was dressing up in colours, everyone had a water gun soaking each other and throwing what I think was white flour on each other. Very random but great fun nursing a hangover. I remember even now, walking through with Jade and water hitting us, it was quite refreshing and just what we needed. We blinked, and then we were back home.

Summer 2016 – My Setback but I Bounced Back. I Guess We Both Did

As we arrived back home, unfortunately, I was made redundant, or should I say the business collapsed while I was away on holiday, which I had an idea about, but this clearly still didn't stop me and Jade going off to Thailand to live the dream again for two weeks and our best adventure yet. So, redundancy had struck twice, and again I hit rock bottom with it all. But they do say it's not how hard you can hit, it's about how hard you can get hit and keep moving forward, it's how much you can take and keep moving forward, that's how winning is done. OK, I'm a Rocky fan. Ha ha ha.

Jade was there to support me and look after the bills for that month until I found my feet again. But I already had a business consultant role in Vitality who I was familiar with anyway due to the businesses I had previously worked for, and I thought this is the next step for me. I got the interview two days after being made redundant and got the job. Working from home and covering south York's and Midlands area, working with IFAs mortgage brokers, and wealth management firms. This was my chance to really understand the market and a fresh start for me. Jade was there 1,000% again to support me as she believed, always, I was destined for massive things, and I think we both felt and believed this, we both were. I went down to London for a whole week for my training, which was bloody intense, but I passed with flying colours and was ready to train and promote Vitality within businesses across the country. Jade even got the train down and spent two nights with me and lined some of her meetings up while I was at HO training and we would spend the evening together, so cute. We went and had Jamaican food and Vietnamese at the Tower Bridge and just watched the world go by. Jade always said to me this is a stepping-stone for you again, but I believe this is what you need and us both working from home, our lives are complete. She was already expecting breakfast made daily etc., I was like, slow down, Pupy, lol. The point is, I had hit rock bottom three times and fell into deep depressive/unhappy states and Jade was always there to pick me right back up, nobody knows this at all; I guess I was too proud to talk about it, I guess I was bothered about what people thought. Well, not anymore. The truth will set you free. Always will, and here I am finding the strength to write about this in this book.

Because Vitality were focused around health and wellbeing, I really started to be mindful of this, and my 2017 journey really opened up a huge fitness journey that will stay with me for life. I used to go out for runs and always listen to motivation music, speeches, people's philosophy on life. This inspired me, but also the background music did and the motivation talks, which going forward and in time only made me stronger but made me bounce back and keep bouncing back. I've always had this faith and hope and believed me and Jade were destined for massive things.

The summer arrived, and we had such a lovely garden, Jade made it look amazing, with all the flowers and plant pots, and we got some new rattan furniture and an umbrella and swinging chair which was Jade's favourite. It was just lovely sitting out having a gin. We also loved a walk around the village, heading for the canal and also West Stockwith Marina.

Was a Baby on the Horizon or Back Travelling Again?

It was June-July time, and Jade decided to have the coil out, this was a very sensible approach as planning a family was the last major step for both of us. Three days after Jade had the coil out, she conceived, which I was happy about, still had good swimmers, they did me proud. My pals used to joke about this to me, saying, "James Guy, your cousin, was going ten to the dozen doing butterfly." Personal joke really and quite funny. James my cousin is an Olympic swimming champion, so that's where the joke came from. I remember Jade on the toilet saying, "Pupy, come in here, look at this. I'm pregnant, wtf, so quick." We couldn't believe it. That summer also I was heading to Magaluf for my cousin's stag do, and always remember walking down to the beach one early morning for sunrise and remember looking out to sea with a tear in my eye, feeling something massive is happening, Jade is giving birth to our child, chills hit my spine. Jade was six or seven weeks into her pregnancy and, unfortunately, she had a miscarriage, we were devastated, and Jade was shook up a lot, I comforted her. We went out and bought a new sofa and also dining table as Jade wanted this. For about one month she didn't really want to get out of bed, but I was there to support and help her bounce back, which I know I did a great job with and I'm so glad she recognised this and told me; I felt I had this ability to help people bounce back just like Jade. Four weeks later, Jade was on the phone to her sister talking about Thailand, and she had told them all about our magical journey earlier on in the year. I think they wanted to experience our trip and also Jade really wanted to show them our footsteps. So that was that; it was November time, and we had booked again to do the same trip, but slightly different hotels. We went in April 2017 this time, so it was a little rainier but still was one hell of a trip. 2017 was a year full of holidays as Jade did seven countries, I think. I forgot to mention also Jade really wanted a cat, so on my birthday 2016, we headed to Bawtry cat sanctuary where Jade picked a cat, but before we go on, I had a fear of cats and thought *How am I going to live with a cat*? But the love I had for Jade, she got her own way most of the time, so there we were choosing a cat on all days, my birthday, I thought I must be mad. Jade chose the cat she wanted it was called Noel, but he arrived at the house Jan 2017, and we called him Rocky, inspired by my pal Pedro's cat also being called Rocky. I won't go into too many cat stories but, short story, I couldn't pick him up, let him jump on me or cross the stairs with him. Ha ha ha ha ha. So, in a nutshell, I was fucked regarding walking naturally and with ease around my own house. Then I released, *What have I done?*

The first of January hit, and I remember even though I was overweight at the end of 2015, nothing much changed end of 2016, and I remember we all had a gathering at my dad's on the 1 Jan 2017. I stepped on the scales and my brother Andy and my dad looked over, and it was 15 stone 11 pound in 2016, but also was like 14 stone-plus start of 2017. I was like *Jesus, man, I best get my groove on; otherwise I will be having an early heart attack at this rate.* I then shared my goal with everyone, and when a goal is shared, with me, more than likely, I will execute it in some way, shape or form. So that was that; I started running properly for the first time.

January flew in 2017 as I was adjusting to Rocky being in the house. It was like hide and seek, but I was always looking for Rocky, although I did start to warm to him and I think deep down he loved me and wouldn't leave me alone, and Jade secretly hated it as she craved for attention, and he just would not give her it. Although he did like a good snuggle in bed sometimes with Jade. I remember I used to come up and there they were, both looking at me with so much innocence, and Jade would normally say, "When's breakfast ready, Pupy?" looking at me with her large blue crystal eyes. My running was coming on also although my first run was 2km and I was breathing like I had smoked 40 fags a day, it was a wakeup call. I had set myself a goal to run my first race, and it was a bloody half-marathon, don't do things by halves, and I had 10 weeks to train for it.

Jade bought me two tickets to Harry Potter World, so she also came with me in February, she was never into Harry Potter, neither was I until I watched all of them in a whole day. When we went, I think she had more fun than me, getting on the video set, buying the photos, and getting into the interaction. She watched the first one with me on that evening and said its quite good, I'm not really into magic, but she liked it. I remember us sat in the

Potter House drinking Butter Beer. Jade had her long black and white coat on as it was a little nippy, she looked like she was in Hogwarts. Anytime me and Jade were in a car together, she would always hold my hand as I put it out, and also she would massage my head and neck, a touch that will never be replicated. She used to send me into a trance with her touch, and it made me shiver from head to toe in a split second. She used to do it all the time. Sometimes I would think bloody hell I'm going to fall asleep here, so used to tell her to stop. "That's enough, Pupy." So, as you can imagine, I was driving home from Watford, driving like Chevy Chase to Walley World. Ha ha ha. Asleep at the wheel.

March came around, and it was time for the Retford half with my brothers, I had lost a huge 1 stone and 7 pounds in 10 weeks from diet and running hard doing 15–18km and many of them. It's all about diet, the 80/20 rule is so true, always will be. You can never outrun a bad diet ever. I clocked a time of 1hr and 53 minutes and was impressed to say my weight in January and the dedication I gave to running for 10 weeks. Jade was so impressed, cheering us on, and as she would say, "I'm so proud of my Pupy." I was in amazing shape, felt great and was gearing up for Thailand again with Jade.

Back to Thailand – We Love You Long Time

April came round so quick, at this time I had left running the telesales department for a healthcare broker as the business had declined and gone into liquidation, and I was nine months into a new business consultant role for Vitality Health and Life, working with IFAs brokers, mortgage advisers across the Midlands and Yorkshire. This role I loved as it was based from home, all expenses paid, and I was building my business up and establishing myself quite well in Vitality amongst the franchises. I was a go-getter, driven and always willing to knock down walls, so sales was always going to be a great area in business for me to explore and thrive within. Jade's work was going amazing, and she was pretty much in the top 5–10 most important individuals in the business without a doubt, and was playing a huge part in the growth and management of the business's current strategies etc. As we were both working from home, this meant so much flexibility for both of us. Anyway, enough talking shop, me and Jade were packed for another great holiday ahead of us, but even though we had the pleasure of having another great holiday in Thailand, I felt it was meant to be for Sally and Rob to see and follow our footsteps on our 2016 trip as this was Jade's best yet.

We were all heading to London with about five boxes of stone-baked pizzas from Retford as Mr and Mrs Piverick, I think they were called, were at the Idle Valley tap, and Jade used them for Sally's hen party the year before. So, it was a pizza pit stop and then London airport. All in all, the trip was a fantastic one. Jade had got to share with her sister what was her favourite tour and route of Thailand, although I felt we should have stopped at Koh Ngai instead of Koh Lanta so they could have experienced the emerald cave, but something told me Jade didn't want her sister doing that as it was very dangerous. We stopped in some memorable resorts, the one in Trang was pretty up there, and also Idyllic surprised us on Koh Lipe. It was amazing to go back to Lipe as they had developed the area, as there was a new beach club and a few more bars that had opened, but me and Jade looked at each other and thought this will be Phi Phi soon, so even now will it be the same. I think it will be even more commercial but still would love to go back. We also went to Koh Rok, which was new for everyone and also stopped at Krabi for a few nights at the same resort as last time, Railay Bay beach resort. What was going to happen on our last night there could never have been predicted. We all got ready for the evening and headed for the walking street where we hit the first bar, so after our first drink, I decided to get a joint and the girls decided to get a space cake, they clearly didn't know what they were asking for or what was even in this cake, but they started diving into it like it was real cake. I thought this night is going to be one to remember, although I was pretty out of it and out of practice with weed, as used to smoke it at uni now and again. (469 boys, ha ha.)

So, the cake was pretty much smashed and so were me and Rob. We all started to waddle down towards the bars and east side of Railay, to then find ourselves in a small bar, stoned out of our heads, drinking a cocktail, feeling pretty paranoid and also laughing our heads off really loud, and obviously was thinking everyone was looking at us. I kept on saying to Jade and Sally, just think what level you are on now, there's another 2–3 levels to go first. They were like "Oh no" and really couldn't handle it, but it was hilarious and moments that will always stay with us all. We then, still were laughing our heads off, wandered down to the Thai boxing event and drank some more alcohol, and all I can imagine now is Jade laughing out loud and so stoned it's untrue. We all found our way back home thanks to Rob and were nursing a very bad hangover in the morning where we had to get a longtail boat, taxi, plane, another taxi and then arrived at the Banyan Tree in Bangkok around 3pm. I just remember us in the pool, still hanging, getting free massages. I couldn't get off the toilet for some reason but had lost all the weight I had gained during the holiday, so bonus springs to mind. That afternoon, we booked in at the sky/rooftop bar and restaurant which sat like a ship on top of the hotel. This was very upmarket and posh, but we deserved it after a great trip. I remember Jade had her long dress with diamonds on, and I had my blue duck shirt on. Jade's tan actually was much better than 2016, I thought, which she was super happy about. Jade has this knack of going on holiday and leaving her fake tan on, then it wears away after a few days and then she starts to tan slightly and then it's home time. This year she learnt not to do this, so I guess that's why.

We were all dressed up and had some photos high up facing out to the city and also some great photos around the table. I remember me and Jade ordered the fresh fish platter and a drink each and I think it was around £300 for both of us, a very expensive establishment I must say, but looking back glad we experienced this together. We had spent so much over the course of the trip, just didn't think we would smash £300 on a meal to end the holiday, as it all went on the credit card anyway. Me and Jade did live life on the edge, and over the years, she rubbed off on me, to enjoy the present and let the future take care of itself. I was more focused on our future and building something for us both etc. I suppose that's why we were like glue; our own qualities together became immensely powerful. I looked out at Bangkok from the bar and thought this place makes me just stop in life, thinking about work, life back home, and makes me feel truly in the present and so relaxed. 2015, 2016 and now 2017, I would like to say we are experienced Thailand travellers having now done around 15 islands. The holiday was coming to an end, and Jade and Sally thought they would go out for a massage across from the hotel two hours before our flight check-in at the airport. Me and Rob were waiting for ages, and eventually they showed in a rush, although I was pretty mad at Jade as we had like two hours to boarding, I think, and you normally have to be there three hours before. Their story was they turned up at the wrong place so had to go on a detour. Anyway, Jade scooped her clothes into her backpack and off we went, another eventful Thailand trip over. Jade was so pleased she had shown her sister Koh Lipe and loved every minute.

Jade was never a big reader, but over the years, I got into my positive energy books and also some biographies. I had years ago read all the *Secret* books and many more, and actually some of the info in those books make so much sense, and positivity, and finding a way to visualise, believe and achieve worked for me. I had one of the *Secret* books and got through half the book, I think, I had already read it, but the *Secret* books were good to go back to as it allowed me to self-reflect on how I have changed and what I've done differently etc. I used to also just open up a random page and read a random line out to Jade sometimes, then close it. Jade read *The Secret*, and she loved it.

I knew our next huge step forward was trying for a baby again, but I didn't want to talk to Jade about it till the end of summer. Jade always had this dream of having a little girl and calling her Daisy. We had arrived back home, and we were straight at it with work, I also had another half-marathon coming up, which I didn't even train for after my Retford half-marathon back in March. I did the half-marathon at Scunthorpe in just under two hours, which wasn't too bad in terms of running memory etc. as

I had two months off running at least, but they do say rest and recovery is key.

Vegas Baby

Business was going very well for me as I had a record quarter for bonus. It was pretty much my first five-figure salary that month, which was a great achievement for me, and Jade was also smashing it in terms of her deadlines and bonus agreements in place. Our next travelling trip was Las Vegas in August for Jade's dads 60th bash, and this was one hell of a holiday, one of my favourites to date. We arrived at Las Vegas, and Jade had organised a limo to pick us all up for the start of her dad's birthday. It was a great surprise for him, we all were sipping bubbly while entering Vegas at sunset, so perfect timing. I couldn't believe what I was seeing, Vegas was truly spectacular. The Vdara where we stayed was a new hotel, its newest built, I think. It didn't have a casino on site, but that was OK. Me and Jade had just been paid our bonuses so really wanted to go all out on the holiday and just live the dream and spend what we want. We had a budget of about 3k to spend, that's if we went crazy, which we did a little. We found an amazing breakfast Mexican restaurant outside of Planet Hollywood, looking over the road at the Bellagio. Jade just loved her pancakes and syrup and also steak and eggs. I remember seeing the Muhammad Ali monument in Bellagio, made me feel the resilience that me and Jade showed for each other over the years, lives about jumping over the obstacles together but coming out even stronger and a more binding force, and this was me and Jade through and through. The highlights of Vegas were that we won 1,000 dollars at Caesar's Palace, which paid for our helicopter ride to the Grand Canyon, and that was a night to remember Jade. We had dropped on our feet as the week we were in Vegas it was the McGregor vs Mayweather fight at the 02, and on that evening the streets were flooded with Irish, but only five hotels had the license to show the fight. MGM held all the cards really, and it was $150 to just walk into the hotel and watch the fight, no bloody chance. Rob had a plan, and he got the fight through his iPad somehow, so we put it on our table in a bar downtown, the girls had gone to watch Britney Spears. As us guys were watching the fight on the iPad, we then turned around, and there must have been about 20 guys behind us looking over our shoulders offering to buy us a pint. Funny moment. I remember Jade and Sally running in like little teenagers after seeing Britney and quite drunk. Jade's smile just beautiful, she was so happy, and I just loved it when she was, nodding at each other like dogs again, in love, Pupy love. That night, Jade went on a dancing bull, we drank so much, gambled and won. The helicopter ride was insane and how we took off and also the views across the canyon and dam was amazing to see. We all had our flying gear on, and we had the helicopter to ourselves which was so cool, and the guy was so informative, I think we tipped him like $40. We stopped off in the canyon for champagne brunch and set back off 10 minutes later as it was too hot, it reminded me a little of *Superman 3*. Ha ha ha, with my black Superman hat on. Jade always said get that off, but I liked it, so I wore it. One thing Jade and Sally were talking about was their parents renewing their wedding vows, and they came around to the idea over drinks around the pool. That was that; they were set for renewing their vows. Rob found a great spot near the Stratosphere, and that evening we all got dressed up and headed for the chapel. When we arrived, it was like something out of an American series on Netflix, we all walked into the chapel, and it was so white, there was a little man at the front who would renew the vows, but we were all stood there laughing our heads off, then Julie walked in with John at the front. Was this really happening? Yes, but also it was a lovely thing to do to celebrate their love as they were also childhood sweethearts. A video was created, and they had photos outside, John was a little drunk, which made the experience even more funny. When Jade was looking back at the video, she always belly-laughed as it looked like I was playing the piano for them at their vow renewal, funny times. Oh, that was it, just came to me, Daniel walked his mum down the aisle and gave her away to John, just hilarious.

I remember also experiencing old Vegas with Jade, as we saw all the cast for the *Walking Dead*, and also decided to stand on the scales at Heart Attack Grill, you had to be over 300 pounds to get free food, but at least we could see what weight we had put on during Vegas. It was a lovely time, just us holding hands and exploring.

The Stratosphere was one hell of an experience, the views and rides at the top were madness, we all enjoyed a nice alcohol slush at the bar and took some pretty amazing pics of the views, and I think we bought a photo from the merchandise shop. I remember I bought a great pic of the helicopter experience and told Jade I will give this to your dad for his birthday.

Vegas was over, and it was one hell of an experience, other than being a stone heavier, lol. Jade always said on the way home one of her favourite highlights was the pit stop at Chicago where we all got Chicago pizzas, and OMG these were something else, food heaven as they say. We were still officially on our holidays so bollox to the diet, I had run like 200km in eight months, didn't care really. I remember flying home. Jade was asleep, sucking her thumb, and the flight attendant came over and served me a drink, I remember her saying, "Aw, look at her, she's sucking her thumb." Trust me, it was the cutest most beautiful thing to see Jade asleep sucking her thumb.

So Many More Trips...

We landed back in the UK, with so much to look forward to and work was getting even better for both of us. I had a planned a 469 reunion in Doncaster with the boys, which was a top night, the boys loved good old Donny; always felt like a holiday when coming to Donny drinking due to so many bars like Magaluf in the summer, so they said, lol. Also, we organised a great bash at Market Rasen races for Jade's birthday with all her family and friends and got a minibus, everyone was hammered, and the sun was shining, a good few winners also. We also got to see Olly Murs show after the races, Jade loved him as she met him and looked after him a whole day when he came to Meadowhall for the lights switch-on. I kept on saying, "He will remember you, Jade." She was drunk, shouting, "Olly," and I never forget the pile-on the girls did, never seen anything like it but, trust me, everyone was smashed, what a day and night.

A few days after Jade's birthday we travelled to Italy to see an old friend and visited Venice, Trieste, Slovenia and Croatia all in three days; this was an amazing break away, and memories created that will always stay.

September 2017 hit, and we were talking about trying for a baby again, Jade had the coil back out, as we did things properly when it came to contraception. It was the end of September, and we got a call off Jade's good friend Louise, who was also family effectively as this was the daughter of my dad's partner, the reason how they got together really; great work by Jade and Louise on this 100%. Jade came down the stairs from having a snooze in the bed, and she said we have been invited to go to Turkey for the week stopping at Lou's partner Sam's place. This was not to be missed, so again we said bollox to it, let's go. Rocky was like a gypsy at the cat home. Turkey turned out to be an amazing trip even though the town was quiet it didn't matter, it was incredible. Now me and Jade arrived at Sam's villa in Turkey before Sam and Lou, and OMFG when we turned up and opened the door, I even did a video, we couldn't believe what we saw; a true MTV cribs pad with a huge infinity pool out to sea, it was something else. The place could bloody host *Love Island*, it was magical. We were blessed to be asked to come and spend time with such an amazing couple. There was like eight bedrooms, I think; we had the first floor, and Lou and Sam stayed at the top where there was like an apartment on the top of the villa. The view when waking up was breathtaking, and this just topped what was probably our busiest year for holidays and success in work etc. Jade had done Iceland with the girls, Thailand, Las Vegas, Italy and now Turkey. We had truly done 2017 in style; it was our best year yet, I think, other than our wedding. Back to Turkey, we did a boat trip one day which was pure pimp style with a bar on board, dinner made for us, and pit-stopped at islands and jumped in the sea off the boat. We also went onto a mud beach where it was really good for skin, getting back into the water with all the mud on. I can't explain what it feels like when you run your hands through your hair and face, so soft and fresh, it's crazy. I remember we got on this dingy hanging off the back of a boat, this took our stomachs a little, and was such a relaxing day. We had created so many memories even to being the only people in the club dancing away at night, where Jade would go on the swing inside, yeah they had a swing in the club, and also this little man who was selling nuts looked so cute, so Jade said, so we gave him £5 for a bag of nuts, and he danced with us. He reminded me of my grandad, Guy, to be honest. What me and Jade thought was absolutely amazing value was £25 PP and people came in and cooked your food, served it, and cleaned your kitchen. Banging value and tasted so good, we did this twice; one was a meat platter, and the other was fish and chips. Another truly amazing holiday that put the cherry on the top of the year. I never forget one evening we went drinking in the town and sat on a rooftop and had porn star martinis, and beers and I told Lou and Sam the brief story of when I went back in my life and fought for what was right, wanting Jade back. I remember Lou having tears coming down her eyes, and Sam nearly went also, it will always be a touching real-life story. After I told them, Jade hugged me and said, "And I'm so glad."

Life Felt Complete

We arrived home, and two days after we had been back, Jade didn't feel right so she took a pregnancy test and it was positive; we hugged on the landing and said to each other this is our time, everything will be OK, trust me. The final piece of the jigsaw had been created, and the picture looked pretty spectacular. Jade remained calm or tried to in the first few weeks of pregnancy, although I'll never forget the time when she threw up in the Co-op, it was like 12 eggs had splattered all over the floor, but she was all good after a sleep. We also went for a private scan around 6–7 weeks as Jade wanted to be sure everything was all OK at this point and it was. I will always remember the time when the letter came through the post for our 12-week scan, and guess which bloody day it was – my birthday 28th December, how mad is that?

Well, it was an amazing birthday gift to be told at 12 weeks, baby Hart is fit and well and so is Mummy, although Jade had a little high blood pressure at the start of pregnancy but nothing major. It came to the end of the year, and I decided to leave my current role at Vitality as a BDM and go self-employed, setting up as a broker with a single tie to Vitality. So, doing this myself, I saw a gap in the market, and I wanted to take advantage of this, so I jumped high and long and quit my employed role for self-employment at the start of 2018. Some thought I was mad for doing this, due to Jade being pregnant etc. I felt it was my time, so I did it. Jade backed me all the way and believed I could do it. I wanted to create a better lifestyle for me and Jade and baby Hart and being bogged down under someone else's rules and expectations just wasn't for me anymore, I was out of employed work for good.

I remember sitting down during October-December really thinking about this decision, and Jade said, "I am here to support and back you all the way." Fear crept in and kept on creeping in, but I made a wise and strong choice to take the leap of faith and do what I had always dreamed of, being my own boss, and working for myself. I always had this poster in my office, which showed a guy leaping from one platform to another, hope and faith it said. So, I made the climb and jumped. I was always very driven, and it led from the heart. My office showed this, as I had and have just images of family members doing great things, to James Guy my cousin becoming world swimming champion, to my brother Neil Hart becoming CEO of Burnley FC, to my sister and brothers on their runs and medals around their necks, to famous positive quotes from Rocky Thierry Henry, and in the corner my symbol, the Superman symbol. S is for hope if nobody knew, lol.

Jade was also getting quite stressed at work at the beginning of 2018, I suppose new targets etc. She felt the pressure, so her bosses decided, due to her pregnancy, they would help with her workload, and created different strategies to ensure Jade could put her laptop down at 5pm and have her evenings to herself. More importantly, I was home, being self-employed, and could be there for Jade pretty much when she needed me, which was priceless and amazing for Jade as it was like she had her own butler services with me. Trust me when I say this, but I was happy that I could be there for Jade.

Off we went again on holiday at the end of January 2018, and you can certainly see a trend here, we spent a lot, we earned enough at the same time, so could do all these lovely holidays. This time it was Cyprus at Jade's Aunty Kim's place. Me and Jade stayed at Kim's place, and Jade's folks stopped at the swanky hotel down the road on the seafront, which was only about two-minutes' drive anyway. We hired a car, so we had freedom on the roads, and Jade was taking it steady, although I remember she did bloody amazing on one trek we made across the seafront, most restaurants were closed but it was a lovely walk. I look back now and think, *Why did I go on this holiday?* I had just started self-employment and should have really said no, and Jade knew this, but I thought *Life's too short; I want to be with Jade*, so I did. I'm so glad I went to Cyprus.

We spent a lot of time at the hotel resort where Jade's parents were, having access to the spa and also pool area. Very nice place it was and felt quite exclusive, I guess it was February so to be expected. We drove to so many places, Paphos Castle, Limassol, and a few other spots. It was just the break we needed, and Jade felt fine and fit and healthy, so we were all good. On our return, we came home to a letter from the NHS to inform us of our 20-week scan, which was all the big reveal as this is when we would find out what sex the baby would be, and we both agreed we wanted to know. The date that was on the NHS letter was just staggering. Jade said to me, "You can't write this, Ric, what's going on?" When we opened up the letter, it said 14th February, Valentine's Day, the time we met, and now it's the day we find out if a boy or girl is entering the world and making our life complete. How could the NHS select the date of my birthday and also the date we met, in terms of us, the 12-week scan and also the 20-week scan. What were the odds? Anyway, it happened, and this was meant to happen like this for us. We believed in fate, and it was amazing.

Baby Hart

The day we went for the 20-week scan, we headed for the hospital and had the scan, the lady just came out with it, and didn't really create a build-up that Jade wanted, she just said, "Do you want to know? It's a boy," very quickly. We couldn't believe it, a little Ric entering the world. Jade was always set on a girl called Daisy, but she just was so set on this little boy being a mini-me looking like a little monkey. We had the day off, so we decided to celebrate with afternoon tea in Retford near the registrar's office, the tablecloth was even blue for us, and also it had an M behind us on a banner for someone reason in terms of where we sat. We kept on sending images to people saying guess the sex, some got it right with the blue cloth. We then headed to Jade's family on the evening to reveal the sex, which was done through a balloon with Baby Boy on, and everyone cheered the house down. Deep down, I wanted a boy, heard too many stories about girls being a handful, and always good having a boy, I thought we can do boy things and enjoy it. We also organised a 4D private appointment to see our baby boy, and the only date available they had was 6 April 2018. Me and Jade looked at each other and thought, you can't bloody write this, our anniversary date. It was all meant to be.

Our next step was choosing a name, but this took time, and we decided to use an app, which worked if we swiped on liking the same name. It was a topic of conversation at night, as I was busy writing business/personal protection and private healthcare for Vitality and Jade was pretty much working from home. I just loved though how we were together most of the time and found times to go for walks and nice meals out, and also had breakfast and tea always together. Jade was also planning a trip to Paris which I had my concerns about, and the doctors advised her not to go, but she still bloody went, she did take it easy, but she was bursting. I always remember looking at an image of her sat near the Eiffel Tower, and she looked huge. So, in the last 12 months, Jade had visited Iceland-Thailand-Las Vegas-Italy-Turkey-Cyprus-Paris, it really was her best year for holidays, which she lived for. I also took another trip out to Italy to spend some time with friends for the weekend in May. Always talking to Jade as she felt speaking to me a good few times a day made her feel better and me also, anything to make Jade feel good/better I did, to be honest. Of course, she was pregnant, and I loved looking after her, being at her beck and call. In Italy, I remember sitting in a restaurant in Venice, and I was drinking apple spritz and saw the name Hugo on a menu, and I knew this was in our top 3–5 names, as there was Theo, Leo, Hugo, Oscar, or Alexandro. I was making jokes to Jade saying let's call him Valentino Hart due to when we found out the sex and also when we met, but she was having none of it. Going back to this menu, when I looked at Hugo as its actually a cocktail, right at that split second, I was like *Wow! That's his name; our little Hugo.* I called Jade up and said let's go for Hugo, she said done deal. Funny how when I looked back at our WhatsApp, she had listed 10 names back in February, and put Hugo in block capitals, just pure madness really, and also our engagement party at Hugo House; was this fate? Was this inevitability?

Pregnancy for a woman is obviously massive and is always a journey, and of course, it can be very stressful and hormonal and certainly was for Jade. Because I had gone self-employed at the beginning of 2018, it was truly amazing in terms of me prioritising my time and not having to slog out 40-hour weeks and spend more time with Jade but also to be there for her as much as I could. Some funny moments, which I'm sure most pregnant woman can relate and what us guys need to just accept, is there isn't a pill which takes all the worries and strains away during pregnancy, it's a rocky road and also an emotional one, and was for Jade. She even at one point used to say, "Ric, just get away from me. I can smell your skin from like two metres away, leave me alone." And also, "You're just pissing me off. Move!" I personally just found it all funny and laughed it off. When Jade just wiggled her finger or gave me a nod while sucking her thumb, everything was perfect again. I guess any argument or bicker we had, when we did our sign language to each other, any worries or troubles just disappeared because it always took us back in our minds to when we were 18–21 years old. At 18–21 years old, you have no worries or issues in life really, nothing is holding you back, and that's where we placed ourselves together in our minds, in great times and also in tough times. Pupy Love.

Jade Was Ready to Give Birth

I remember our local restaurant in the village was doing a Thai night, so we booked in, this was an amazing meal and took us back to all our special spots and places. We decided to walk home, and Jade got tired, so I went and got the car and came back to pick her up, she did a video for the girls also, as she was waddling big time. Jade's due date was 4 July 2018, and the date was coming round quick. I remember Jade woke up on the Monday of the week commencing 2 July and said she couldn't really feel Hugo. Probably a little worry more than anything, I thought, but she said she wanted to go and get checked out. So that's what we did, heading for the hospital early that week, for Jade to be checked over. Everything seemed OK with Hugo, but Jade had developed high BP, which was being managed with BP tablets that she needed to take, ready to be induced Friday 6 July. It was World Cup time and England at the time were rocking and doing so well, it felt like Euro 96 with the passion flying around the nation.

Thursday 5 July, Jade enjoyed a lovely day out with her mum, going to a lovely pub local to us and sitting out enjoying the sun and had an appointment to be checked over at Retford Hospital with her BP, which all went to plan. I had already wound down with work and being as proactive as possible. My diary had been marked out for at least two–four weeks after birth. I was also, behind the scenes, taking steps to set up my own healthcare brokerage Hart Health, as I felt my current setup was only dinting my earnings and didn't feel I was getting enough from my current umbrella. It was inevitably the next step anyway. I was very excited about this, and so was Jade.

We had been told to call up triage the Friday morning at 7am and then head straight into the hospital, but when we called that Friday, they had told us to hang fire for most of the day due to capacity and business on the labour ward. So, we decided to go to the Pantry for breakfast and enjoy the morning of the start of our most exciting journey together. Jade ordered a purple sunrise shake, and also some dragon fruit cheesecake, and I got a gym fix breakfast. We also got some photos taken; I have no idea why, but the girl working there took some pics of Jade, which was very random but extremely lovely and thoughtful. We went back home as all the bags were prepacked in the car with everything we needed and headed to the hospital at 2pm as they said it was OK to come along. Jade got onto a bed on the A2 ward about 4pm-ish and doctors were checking her BP, while I was there by her side, having the iPad there to watch the World Cup wearing my England top. Jade really enjoyed the food on the ward as it was mainly jackets with tuna, or cheese and beans and this was heaven food for her. She always demolished all the food and also the pudding, of course. She used to look up at me, licking her lips and say, "Pupy, you can go to the canteen, I'm busy eating all this food," it was so funny. Jade stayed overnight on the A2 ward on the Friday. I ended up going back home late and got some sleep to then arrive back very early in the morning on the Saturday. I got some breakfast in the canteen and headed to the A2 ward. That morning, we took a walk around the hospital, not going to far, but we took a walk into the shop, looking at baby clothes hanging from the shop front, and also Jade bought some more crisps and sweets etc. The weather was amazing, so we went outside for a while and sat on the grass. Jade had my shades on, looking gorgeous as ever with her yellow and blue floral dress on. She got her phone out and started playing 'Don't Worry Baby' by the Beach Boys and, she said to me, "This is so lovely. Beach Boys, sun shining, sat out on the grass with my Pupy." I told Jade I loved her more than life itself; always have done, always will and can't wait for our bundle of joy to arrive – that being Hugo – making our lives perfect in all ways. We looked at each other, nodding our heads while she was sucking her thumb, stroking her nose. We had got to this point, and the way I felt about Jade had never changed since we were young and vice versa. If anything, our love grew, we never moved away from our love as kids together, and the way we both felt at 18 years old, and that's the beauty of love, right. So many people break up, lose sight of the person you are with, and most of the time, this is due to work, changes, communication and also financial issues, or not working as a team and understanding your role in the partnership/relationship. But these are just factors that get in the way, and why should they stamp on the most important thing, which is love.

Me and Jade when went to bed always had this certain lock we did, which we did at 18 years old and it never changed or broke, I suppose subconsciously, at night, we were always 18 years old, Jade by my side would just go straight to sleep. I always said to Jade, not all the time but in bed, "Growing old with you is a dream, that's the most important thing." I remember always when I was driving somewhere or being somewhere else without Jade, and I thought of her, I would say out loud in my car mainly, "Jade, I just love you so much; you're my Pupy," in our funny voice, the way we spoke to each other, like puppies, I guess. We just loved each other through and through, a bond unbreakable really. We got up off the grass on that Saturday 7 July and headed back for the ward as it was around 2–3pm. When we arrived back on the A2 ward, I remember something wasn't working on my iPad, and I was missing the England and Sweden game, which was the quarters of the World Cup. I remember asking one of the nurses if she knew where it may be on in the hospital. She came back to me and whispered both of you come with me, so we followed this nurse into a private pregnancy room, with a TV on the wall, a sofa, kitchen etc., and me and Jade sat down on the sofa while the midwives would wander in or stay in the room watching the game with us. Jade was really comfy and no pain at this stage, which was good news, so we sat back and watched the match. All the midwives were playing games and bets on how many calls they would get re woman going into labour during the football match, most of the midwives stayed in the room for the majority of the game. Jade was on her phone, talking to family and also texting friends but also cheering with me when we scored. England had beaten Sweden in the quarter-finals of the World Cup 2018, and we were heading for the semi-finals. The last time we saw the semis is when it was England-Germany when

Lineker told Bobby Robson to keep an eye on Gazza, we all never forget that caption ever. They didn't get to the final anyway. Jade then went back to her bed on the A2 ward, and I headed to the café for tea, and I got a message from Jade saying they had moved her onto the labour ward finally – around 6.30pm it was – and she was in her pregnancy room. I came in and let Jade get comfy on the bed, and got the room set up for her in terms of snacks and a picnic area near the window, and then also used one of the tables to set up Jade's spa feel she wanted. So, I got all her Neal's Yard products out, which she had brought, and also some tea lights, and placed them all on the table and around her bed, with the iPad nearby where I had all the spa music ready to go. That evening, the midwives came in and checked on Jade and also added the pessary in to get things going with Jade's pregnancy and movements. She was hooked up on the machine, and I used to act like a horse as the heartbeat was like a horse galloping. I stayed with Jade that Saturday evening and slept on the chair and had her purple stomach ball as leverage for my legs to rest on. Jade took a photo of me on her phone, and I looked so uncomfortable. I remember walking around 5am, shattered, so I went back home only till 10am-ish to recharge for the day ahead. Jade slept quite well actually, which I was pleased about. She had her breakfast that morning, I think she asked for jam on toast and orange juice. I arrived back at the hospital for around 11am, and when early afternoon hit, Jade did start to get contractions. We had done a hypnotherapy course, well Jade had, and I went to a couple of sessions, and we had watched a hypnotherapy course online that we bought and would spend half an hour each evening watching it together. I personally wasn't very open-minded about this, but, guys, defo get on this with your Mrs as I got into it and learnt some great techniques to ease stress and also help mummy in pregnancy and hitting certain pressure points depending on the stages of labour. Jade and I were doing some breathing techniques, and I was massaging Jade as much as possible where she was comfortable on the bed. I would use her Neal's Yard oil and massage her feet and legs for hours really that afternoon with the spa music on and the tea lights on, giving her that spa feel. I don't recall many midwives coming in at all to check on Jade that Sunday pm, so it was just us. Her mum and dad came for the day, but also went off for a walk or to the shops but came back to be with Jade up to labour. I remember I had to go out on to the ward and get the ward manager to come and see Jade as no midwives were to be seen. She came in and examined Jade to find out she was 4–5cm already dilated, I was fuming at the midwife as she came in and apologised saying, "Sorry, I've not been around at all." I get she had a huge workload, but management of people is key, end of. It just seems not enough micro-management was happening on the ward and, most importantly, they didn't seem like they were working together. Anyway, it was around 4pm, and Jade's mum was there, and myself and John, I think, around this time went out to the café when Jade started the first stages of labour. I was still massaging her feet, which she wanted me to and was relaxing her in some way. The evening kicked in, and Jade was being seen by more medical specialists; gas and air was on tap alongside various drugs given to Jade. In short, Jade fell into labour around 6–7pm properly, and the baby could come in a matter of 3–4 hours said the midwife.

Jade gave birth to our beautiful little boy at 22.09 on Sunday, 8 July 2018, and he was ours. Jade said when he came and went to her chest, "I can't believe he's ours." We did it! Jade was breastfeeding pretty much straight away, and we didn't want to reveal his name too soon, as I think Jade wanted to wait for her dad to come to reveal his name. Hugo went onto the baby table to just compress his chest and get more oxygen to his lungs then he went back on Jade. Jade and I had 20 minutes quality time together holding Hugo. She was pushed out of the delivery room at 22.50 and taken to surgery for manual removal of her placenta. I called Julie and told her to come with John back to the delivery room, as they were waiting to want to give us time together as a family. We all then sat in the room, waiting for Jade to come back. I was explaining to Jade's parents that they were having issues getting Jade's placenta out and they were doing it manually in theatre. Julie said, "Yes, I had two retained placentas." The night was getting late, and Jade had not arrived back, and we were all worried about what was going on, there was not one midwife or doctor to be seen on the ward.

The doctors came in around 12.30pm to say, "Do you want me to tell you how it is, guys?" to then reveal that Jade had a cardiac arrest, and she was stable in a coma, and told us this was due to drug toxicity. My heart shattered, and my mind went into shock... She was stable; that was the main point as they said, the midwife even said she has the best team around her all working like clockwork. I couldn't believe what I was hearing. I couldn't imagine what was going through Julie's and John's head at this point, but it was like someone had ripped my insides completely out of me, and the whole world stopped, time and everything. I remember walking out the hospital at the back doors, ringing my parents to tell them Jade had a cardiac arrest. I fell to my knees outside and broke into a thousand pieces. All the family then started to travel and arrive at the hospital. Everyone came into the main hospital delivery room on the labour ward. Hugo was having his first black shit, which I think I missed, and he was being held and fed via milk in a cup by family. Jade was at the forefront of my mind, and I prayed to God Jade would be OK and survive. The time hit, it was around 4.35am, and the midwife came in and grabbed my arm and asked for immediate family only to come and took us upstairs as Jade had been moved from theatre to ICU. The midwife wouldn't answer questions I was asking, and as we arrived onto the ward, the doctors informed us that Jade had deteriorated, having had a further four cardiac arrests, and she wasn't going to make it. So there I stood in ICU, my wife had gone, seeing a machine over her in ICU and my baby boy back in the delivery room being held but not by his mummy or daddy. Jade's life came to an end, and I watched them turn the machines off. My Pupy, my Soulmate, my Life had gone forever.

In ICU (Hospital post Jade)

It's now May 2020, and I have no idea how I am finding the strength to write this, but a pandemic has hit the world due to COVID 19, and lockdown has given me heaps more strength and peace with my boy. A book is always something I was going to do, but it was all about the right time, and now is my time to do this for Jade's legacy and also maybe provide some valuable therapy for me. Some may see Jade's legacy as other things, but what I do know right now is this book is absolute and won't change and will be a force in itself, in memory of Jade and for Hugo as he grows up wanting to understand more and will read this and asking Daddy many questions.

I walked out of ICU and back down to the labour ward with my family, although I can't remember at all even walking down to the labour ward. My life had been shattered into a thousand pieces. Jade had died in theatre and ICU and I couldn't believe what I was seeing in front of my eyes; Jade lying there. The next thing I was on the labour ward in a private room, the room where we watched the semi-final of the World Cup. I found a way to climb into bed, it was around 6am, and I remember my body had just shut down for about two hours. All the family were around in the room, I wasn't really in a deep sleep, so could hear them muttering, but my body had fallen into major shock. I woke around 8am and went straight into the shower and just sobbed while the water trickled down me, thinking *What the fuck is going on, Jade has died, why?* My body was still in shock, and I had totally forgotten I had a boy in the hospital, who was being fed by family and the midwives. I couldn't stop crying, and I went back up to ICU to see Jade. I looked outside the window of the hospital, looking over at the field where we sat on the day before delivery, listening to music and talking about our love and life together, and now she has gone. Thoughts that are just indescribable and impossible to comprehend.

Lots of family came over that day, Monday 9 July, all of Jade's friends' group came, and all family on both sides. When each family member came onto the ward, I approached them with open arms as they did with me and took them up to ICU to see Jade. I did this all day about 10 times, and I don't know how, but I felt I wanted to do this, and I just needed to be beside Jade as much as possible. She was my Soulmate, my Pupy, my Life. We only had up to 4pm with Jade for us all to see her. I just couldn't believe what was going on, my head was spinning, I couldn't really talk properly, but constantly in tears every 5 minutes and my body felt like I had been hit by a train 1,000 times over. Just knowing I was walking out of the hospital on my own with Baby Hugo without Jade broke me, and a massive part of me also died on July 8 2018. I remember telling everyone the name of our baby boy, I remember now as I write this, when the doctors told us Jade had passed, I went back down to the delivery room to hold my boy, knowing he would never see his mummy again, broken in every single part of my body and soul. I announced his name to all the family who were in the delivery room as Hugo Jaden Hart; his original name was going to be Hugo James Hart, but I changed this due to Jade passing. Jade didn't know about this, and I did this in memory of her. Jaden was the second on the list for middle names, but Jade was happy for me to use my middle name. I'm so glad I changed this to Jaden.

The next day was a day of silence, with all our family and friends around us. Going up to see Jade lying there and had died was a situation I just can't explain in words, she just seemed asleep to me, which she just loved to do. I guess also I had no idea what was going on, and my world had stopped, and understanding of all that had happened just wasn't being processed in my head, well it wasn't. I guess I was just putting one foot in front of the other literally, in pain, pure pain.

On Monday 9 July, Hugo started to develop a birthmark, which was strange, and it developed into something quite remarkable in terms of the shape, which is on our Insta page (a love heart). Doctors were coming in trying to explain what had happened, which all sounded not very informative and wishy-washy and unclear. Hugo was being given milk by most of the family, and I remember he was sick on my sister, bless him. The doctor came up and told me everyone will need to say their goodbyes to Jade. I went up on my own then also with Jade's friends, which was just heartbreaking. I touched her feet again, giving her a little last foot massage, as I was doing for hours before and up to labour. All her bunions had disappeared, and her feet looked bloody amazing, it was so crazy to see. I just felt she was asleep and would be waking shortly, but she wasn't, she had died straight after birth and had gone forever. I remember looking out of the ICU window again and thinking wtf am I going to do going forward without Jade and our baby boy on my own, my life had been shattered into a million pieces.

Shortly after the last time I could see Jade, the midwives pulled me into a room and were teaching me how to put a nappy on and also how to bath your baby. I was like what the hell is going on, my head was a daze. But I managed to find some light at that moment as I did a short video with Hugo behind me in the bath, singing "Footballs coming home, Hugo's coming home" as England were in the semi-finals of the World Cup against Croatia. I was very upset at the same time doing the video, I haven't shared this one with anyone until now, but it's on my phone.

Tuesday 10 July came, and it was discharge day for me and Hugo, all alone without his mummy or my wife. When I strapped Hugo in his pram seat and carried him out of the hospital, floods of tears came down my eyes. As I walked down the corridor and exited through the doors, the sunlight hit me; I had entered the world going forward without my Pupy and felt so guilty leaving her in the hospital. I felt lost and was starting to lose short-term memory, this did become a problem throughout my grief process, but I'm OK now with memory. I placed Hugo in the car correctly, so I remembered this one from a YouTube video – Jade would have been happy about this – and off I went in the car, heading back home with Jade's mother and sister in the car with me. I recall when driving back to Swallowsnest and hitting certain roads, asking myself, *Where am I? Which is the correct way home?* I remember driving through Worksop and arriving near Gainsborough Road, and I had no idea where I was, looking out to the countryside. The mind is the most powerful thing we and this universe holds, in my opinion, it keeps the world going, and keeps us going. Mine had shut down completely, but I had a boy to feed and take care of, so I needed some reserve, and I found it, this was simply down to some form of inner strength I never knew I had. When I arrived on the drive back at Swallowsnest without Jade, for starters it didn't feel like home anymore. I felt she was still upstairs asleep sucking her thumb, shouting for breakfast, but the house was cold and empty, and she wasn't: she had died and was in the hospital all alone. Rocky was also crying for food, and I was like, *For fuck's sake, the cat needs sorting, and I can't even pick him up*, as I was still nesh around him with my fear of cats.

Hugo needed feeding; it was a good job I had been bought shitloads of on-the-go small bottles of Aptamil for newborns. Looking into Hugo's eyes as a newborn and him looking back at me, snapped my spine in half and ripped my heart out my body, his mummy had died, and I had far too much spinning around my head even after two or three days, the present the future, everything. Jade gone, Hugo without his mummy, me without my soulmate.

A few days later it was the semi-final of England in the World Cup, I don't know why but I invited everyone to my house to watch the game, there wasn't much watching doing, to be honest, I was keeping my eye on Hugo, and everyone was holding him etc. I was outside with my England top on holding Hugo in his England outfit only a few days old with the flag behind me. I was totally not with it, it's like I had left my body completely, and I was just in motion, all I was focused on was feeding Hugo; that was it, keeping my son alive and well. He needed feeding every two hours, and nappy changes, I found it so hard doing his nappies on my own at the start, when it was just like piccalilli and there was bloody shitloads of it. Ha ha ha ha ha. Also, this is so hard to share as I write this, but it came shortly a few days after the semi-final of the World Cup, every time I had Hugo in my arms and every time I was feeding him or even just glancing at him, I would be thinking of Jade's death. Just death came to my head every time I looked at him, which was a lot. And sometimes I had to close my eyes and just breathe and believe and have faith and hope this horrible feeling of death would leave me and my head every time I looked at Hugo. It was one of the hardest things to face mentally, knowing your wife had died, and you didn't even get to say goodbye, and me having suicidal thoughts every day alongside death whacking me in the face every time. Looking at Hugo, thinking of his mummy, was trust me the worst place ever to be placed in.

Hugo loved his sleeping sheep at night, which really helped him, and I also got a swinging electric chair from my sister's friend, which was very kind, and he loved this. The music in the background stays with me and will do forever, even to date, I can't listen to the sheep again, as it does take me back to the first few weeks after Jade. I am very strong, but this is a place I just can't go back to, so friends and family in the future, don't turn on the sleeping sheep when I'm there. Much appreciated.

The next steps were dealing with the coroner and also organising a funeral director and where Jade would be laid to rest. As we lived here in Misterton, Doncaster and only had lived here for three years, I decided Jade should be laid to rest at Ackworth cemetery where all her family members are and very close around all her family tree. Also, I had lots of support from family on both sides, mine and Jade's. They would stay over with me for the first two to three weeks, so I wasn't on my own, which I was so appreciative of, maybe not at the time as I was in a very dark world, but this really helped as I didn't want to be alone. I slept downstairs for weeks with Hugo, on a blow-up bed, and on the sofa, I don't know why. I guess the room had the space and I just wanted all the things around me I needed, and also the milk maker was a godsend. But most of the time I was not even fully awake, and still working out in my head Jade dying and why, alongside dealing with the funeral, alongside having two or three hours' sleep a day, feeding Hugo every two hours and it was getting on top of me. I guess I had been pushed to my limits in my head, psychically and mentally and it was sink or swim. I just wanted someone to come and swipe me off the planet, to be honest, but Hugo was in my mind more, and he needed me. I remember going to sleep one evening about two weeks after Jade had passed, and as I fell asleep, someone grabbed my feet with two hands and started massaging them. This was either my mind being extremely clever, or Jade was touching my feet. I believe it was Jade, as when I said stop it stopped. It was her way of saying to me thank you for massaging me in my last hours, and massages were massive parts of Jade's relaxation and happiness and mine also. I remember also going upstairs to my bedroom, and Jade's favourite clock on her bedside table had stopped. Now everyone can have their take on this, but this clock could have stopped at any time, and it stopped at 10.09 bang on, the time Hugo was born. (Which is on Jade's website.) It was like a message to say when Hugo entered, Jade's life stopped, and it did, unfortunately. Her other favourite clock downstairs had also stopped at 5am, this was the time she was declared dead in the hospital, so why her two favourite clocks stopped at these crucial times, I have no idea, but you couldn't write this. How could this happen, and what are the odds? Also, I fast-forward now to buying Hugo his play kitchen and what time appears on the kitchen clock, his birth time... unreal... It was a message; I believe there are messages always around us; it's just how and what we are tuning into at the time and if we see them.

It had been two to three weeks gone, and Jade had been released to the funeral directors, so me and Hugo headed there straight away, this was a horrific experience for me, and I had to walk into a room where she had been prepared and was lying there. I took some photos where Hugo was in his car seat on the floor near his mummy, my heart was broken, my Pupy had gone. I was still in shock. I still have photos of Jade that will stay with me forever on her own lying there and with Hugo. I also got a photo with Jade and Hugo together in the hospital on the 9 July, but this is a photo I just can't go back to, not a nice one, I don't know why I took it.

I left the funeral directors to arrange all, and I think Jade's sister Sally organised Jade's music, with me giving many songs also and her eulogy. I also went down to the local florist in Ackworth with Jade's family to pick the flowers, I just didn't want to be doing this, and started to get angry inside and it was boiling. It was crazy as about one month before Jade passed, we spoke about death in bed, and I was saying to Jade she would outlive me totally. She said to me, "I couldn't live without you, Ric." This still breaks me now. She always said she wanted a Beach Boys song at her funeral and everyone in summer dresses; the summer dresses were mentioned way back, but the Beach Boys and chat about who will outlive who was three to four weeks before 8 July.

Jade loved 'Good Vibrations' but also 'Don't Worry Baby' (Beach Boys), and she chose to listen to 'Don't Worry Baby' when we were sat on the grass the day before the birth, so this is why I had this played at the funeral. The funeral came round quick, which was 3 August, and was exactly how Jade would have wanted it. It was like she had written this out step by step, so myself and whoever helped me need a massive pat on the back; we did it, we did her proud. My Pupy.

The Funeral of Jade Michelle Hart

It was the night before the funeral, and we were at Jade's family house, Jade was in an amazing vintage style basket I had chosen for her in her parents' dining room, looking out to the garden that she just loved. I spent most of the evening with her but needed some sleep, so I got a few hours. Hugo was asleep, which was good. I said to myself, and in honour of Jade, for the one day of her funeral, I needed to be the strongest I've ever been. The morning came, the flowers around Jade smelt beautiful, I decided to wear my wedding outfit again, and the dresswear for the ladies was summer dresses and red lipstick and the chaps, suits with floral ties. All Jade's family were turning up that morning, the sunrise was amazing to see, but on an extremely hard day, felt like it lasted forever. The hearse, which was all white, came to collect Jade and we all walked behind her on the street up to the church, which was in Nostell Priory National Trust, a place Jade loved always in her heart. Her playground as a child. Well, we were setting her free at Nostell that day. I remember walking behind the car, having my hand on the side of the car, I just felt I needed my hand on the car to feel Jade. We arrived at the church, and most were already in the church. We picked Jade out of the hearse and got her up on our shoulders, it was me, Jade's brother, dad and uncle, I recall. I can't really remember much, but we started to walk in with her, it was like walking into a festival, the turnout was truly beautiful to see and everyone dressed for summer. We placed Jade at the front, and I sat at the front with Jade's family and my own family behind me. I got a few hands on the shoulders, so thank you whoever did that, felt warming and helped. We had some hymns, but also we had the Calling – 'I Will Go Wherever You Will Go' played, also the song on our entrance was our wedding song, 'Thousand Years' – Christina Perri. The time had come, and it was my speech about me and Jade to everyone in the church, I felt I could have stood up there all day, but I prepared some words this time around. I said to myself, I would stay strong, and I wanted to read this freely without tears, but feelings can't be helped, but I did it, I guess I was still in shock. The wheels were slightly moving in my head, but I captured everything that meant so much to me and Jade, and the speech is still in Jade's memory box as I write this. A slogan both me and Jade lived by was "treat every working day like your first and treat every day like your last"; grasp this, and you will have one hell of a life. It even stuck with all Jade's workforce, they decided to place this on their wall at work as a remembrance of Jade, which is just lovely. So, let me just run this by everyone who is reading this right now, I found the strength to stand up in front of everyone and talk about mine and Jade's life together, holding it together pretty well, never judge a book by its cover ever. Some thought I was OK due to no tears or breaking and not being able to read everything, but let me tell you, I was shattered and just didn't know which piece to pick back up; I was just putting one foot in front of the other and in my mind had disappeared from reality and was in a very dark place.

Jade's mother, Julie, also got up and did an amazing speech about Jade and her life as a child and growing up, she did bloody amazing and also stayed extremely strong. This is what I call the force and all the energy of strength coming our way, we had found the strength to stand up in front of everyone four weeks after Jade's passing and talking openly and freely about a beautiful soul. Not easy but we did it; but let me tell you, shock was still very much in my mind. Jade's service came to an end. We pushed her out at the end and walked out with her, with the Beach Boys 'Don't Worry Baby' playing and tears streaming down my eyes, looking up into the sky thinking what the fucking hell is going on, lost, empty, broke, weak, were all happening all at once with major anxiety. A vintage-looking bus we got for the afternoon was waiting to take family only to the wake, which was in a barn building at Farmer Copley's in Pontefract. The wake was more like a wedding celebration, we had a band – Super Sonnets – on in the corner and also pictures of Jade scrolling on screens, with bunting hanging from the beams and also picture frames everywhere, with a sweet shop, and also picture albums of Jade. This, as you can picture, was no normal wake; Jade was no normal girl, her send-off was out of this world. I remember getting around to speak to all, some didn't know what to say, and that's OK, but I was grateful to have all Jade's important family and friends around us and also mine. I recall some people coming up into the room thinking that it was a wedding, and didn't have any idea it was a wake, and many were stood outside and up and down the stairs leading into the main room. We did an afternoon tea for everyone, and it was exactly how Jade would have loved it. Moments that stay with me are listening to the 'Love Death Birth' song from the *Twilight* movie that Jade loved. Also, my Uncle Steve, Dad's brother, saying a prayer for me and Jade with his wife Anne; this brought me to my knees in my mind. I remember drinking quite a lot at the wake, had nearly a bottle of JD to myself, but nobody knew, to be honest, as I couldn't get drunk. Some of my senses and feelings had switched off, I think, within me, so I found I would need to drink double to feel the normal effects of being drunk, but luckily this is one thing I didn't turn to. And I thank my past self for not doing this or taking this path as I write this. I suppose it's always a good feeling when you thank your past self for the decisions made. I would always ask myself, what would my future self be proud of? And I was always like this, and always will be. I could have quite easily turned to the bottle as it took a lot to get me drunk or even hit me, so I could have fallen deep into the bottle, and I saw this happen in my mind but knew I couldn't turn to this or even contemplate it. I'm so proud I didn't do this.

All my friends had come from university and also my old pals from Doncaster, which I appreciated so much. I suppose everyone has their own journey with losing a loved one, but my body had gone into major shutdown and had just enough battery to manage Hugo, but my responses and thought processes weren't normal anyway and had all just disappeared. I remember a photo taken of me and Hugo on the day of the funeral and my eyes are just black with a huge ring of black around them, this was a visual of hell stepping into my life for the next two to three months and going forward. The wake couldn't have gone better for Jade and everyone started leaving, I got a taxi back to Jade's parents. I remember hugging all my family, especially my brother Jay, as I think he knew mine and Jade's true love deep down more than most, I suppose.

Off I went back to Jade's parents, everyone started drinking even more and having pizza etc., but I went straight to bed. I made a conscious choice then that I couldn't let alcohol defeat me, and my boy needed me the next day. I also took many flowers from the funeral and used these to hang in my house off the beams, and it made the room feel very spiritual and made me feel better, smelling the flowers daily until they died. So I hung them upside down as they dried, Jade just loved to do this around the home anyway.

Writing this now is the hardest thing I've ever had to do, as I am trying to piece everything together and remember as much as I can and go to some very dark places, as my brain was in shutdown mode totally. Also, my mind went back to June around two weeks before Jade gave birth. I remembered going out for two half-marathon runs in one week around the third week in June, I was really keeping on top of my running, but was conscious if Jade went into labour, I was like 15 miles away, but it was all OK.

August came round quick, realisation had hit after the funeral, which it does. The aftermath and stepping forward are always the hardest parts as I was still alive with our boy Hugo, having to feed him every two hours and look after him, and just being at Swallowsnest sent me into a very dark place, being all alone in the house without Jade. I would sit in my house alone with Hugo asleep, and that's when you start to panic and worry about what happened to Jade. How was she feeling at the time? Could she understand what was happening? What happened when she died?

Where is she now? These just send you into a very dark, depressive state of panic and major anxiety struck.

I remember sitting at my laptop, typing a word document out, which was my own funeral and exactly how I wanted it to be. I felt I didn't want to live any more. Was I thinking of suicide? Yes, at all angles, I felt at that point there was no way out, even with Hugo. And some may say, but what about your little boy? Well, I found myself at one of the darkest places anyone could have gone to, so there I was typing my funeral out, part by part, without thinking about anyone other than I can't do this, and the world and Hugo will be better off without me, and I wanted to be with Jade. I saved it and shut my laptop and then went and got Hugo a bottle of milk as he was crying. I didn't stay in the house with Hugo on my own till early August, and I remember the first night on our own. I was like shit, I'm on my own, and anxiety and worry hit the roof, and just didn't feel capable at all, frail, weak, and grieving for my Pupy in its worst possible state.

Jades 34th Birthday 15th August

Jade's birthday was coming up, so I decided to host it as a gathering with family and friends at the local Pantry, and we had some Thai food which they cooked up for and sorted the buffet out, which was so helpful and kind. I had some Chang beers as they got some especially for the event. It was so lovely to see everyone again. I remember the owner of the Pantry giving me a margarita that reminded her of Bangkok, and it tasted bloody good. I can't really remember much from Jade's birthday other than these memories, alongside also going back home where I think Jade's family stayed over and I was in floods of tears in the kitchen, and just had no energy left. I went outside and smoked a cigarette – not like me as I had quit a while back in my life, but I wasn't myself, period, and that was OK. The fact of the matter is, something not normal had happened to me losing Jade under the circumstances, so my thoughts were also going to be abnormal. Grief is a journey of knowing you as well and understanding what's right and what matters going forward, I was still in this black hole trying to see any form of light, relying on my inner strength and gut to take me along this journey. It was literally one foot in front of the other, trust me.

Shortly after Jade's birthday, my brother Jay asked me if I wanted to go away to Portugal in September for a few days. This is what I needed, to get away, running away was all I wanted to do, so I accepted the invite, and this break was my turning point in my head or certainly a change in direction in my head and thoughts.

It was also my mum's 60th birthday bash end of August, and she was thinking of cancelling this, I said it goes ahead, we don't stop what we intend to do. The party went ahead, and I dressed as Darth Vader, I suppose I had turned to the dark side, and fighting my way back to the light and finding my inner strength and force again.

Portugal September 2018

I went away to Portugal, and my aim was just to feel a tad lighter than I felt back home, it was more about being out of my four walls as this was still a very dark place for me in terms of my thoughts. A few beers and fresh air and sun were what I needed. I remember on most mornings, I would run down to the beach with music in my head, thinking about mine and Jade's life and Hugo being here now. The music in my ears was all the songs and general motivation that I had in my ears when running during 2016–2018 before July 2018 and all the tunes and themes that drove me before July 2018. I had to find a way back, and also how I felt around getting on top of my thoughts. I remembered when I used to run, I found a way of listening to music, thinking of something and then really feeling it, so tingles would be all over my body from head to toe, like an adrenaline rush, but it was like I was in touch with the universe and felt the ground and environment I was in. (The gravity of energy.)

So, I ran down to the beach in Portugal for the sunrise, still a little pissed, and floods of tears coming down my face as I looked out to the sea, lost, with so much anxiety, thinking *Where are you, Jade, how am I going to live without you?*

It turned out to be quite a boozy weekend, but the final evening will stay with me forever and was my turning point in my head to find a way to climb out this black hole and try and keep my head above water, and I felt some light. I was sat in a bar outside with the boys on the square, and as I sat down with my hands on the wooden table and my beer looking at me, it felt like someone grabbed my left hand and squeezed it tight. I looked at my hand and thought *what the fuck is going on?* Nothing was there, then a second after, a band appeared at the end of the bar, and the words started, 'so lately been wondering, who will be there to take my place,' – it was the Calling 'Wherever You Will Go' (our song). My body shivered from head to toe, and at that moment, I knew Jade was with me and giving me a sign that I can do this. We were both spiritual people and believed in the afterlife, we weren't religious but spiritual. The moment also took me back to two weeks after Jade passed and I went to bed and had the most real dream ever. I had stepped out of my body, looking at myself sleeping, and Jade appeared through my TV and wall, and her face came through, and we kissed, and this kiss felt more real when she was alive. The two moments came together, and then I knew *I will make you proud, my Jade.*

I arrived back home to pick Hugo up, and the death feeling went. I believe this happened because maybe a few days away helped, but also the moment Jade touched my hand, and the Calling came on, on my last night must have triggered something in my head to say *You can do this.* I was so relieved, and I drove home that day with Hugo, with a small grain of hope. It was also a time where Hugo's birthmark had really flared up and was like a 4D heart shape in red on his head, this was a sign for me, as we were the Harts and I believe it was a message from a force outside our control. Remember, it could have been any shape at all in the world, and it was a heart. I believed if Jade could get a sign to me, she would, and she was already doing this. The world and us are made up of energy, and I believe her energy is always around us.

I decided to set up a 10k run in memory of Jade for November for everyone to get involved. I was going to keep Hugo's Just Giving page open for the run but decided to close it. His page reached £17k and I couldn't believe the generosity of so many, I knew I would use this to invest in Hugo's future, and that is exactly what I have done. I gave everyone enough time to train and get ready for the Leeds Run in November, so I started to find time to run while family came and watched Hugo. Now the pain I was feeling was unbearable, and every time I would wake up, I would snap in half then have to get myself sorted and also dressed and feed my boy, with also dealing with my nightmares frequently during the night having only two or three hours' sleep. I recall also waking myself up in my sleep sobbing, then waking and not realising where I was. I wouldn't wish this on anyone in this world. All my anger and feelings would build up each day, and I wanted to remain strong for Hugo and also find a way to find silence amongst people where I just wanted to snap, which could have been quite easily with most friends and family. So I decided to bottle things up and release all this during my runs, and I feel this was the best decision under the circumstances I could have made at this time, otherwise nobody would have wanted to be around me, and this is the truth. And let me tell you, under the situation and circumstances and everything going off in my head, it was the hardest thing to find silence, but I did it, much harder than letting your anger out for sure. (Everyone had their own journey and way of dealing with Jade's loss) Every time I would set off, my body would tingle all over and ache, alongside floods of tears falling down my face, and as stupid as this sounds, I would talk to the universe, the world, a greater god, *Why Jade, why me and Hugo?* Then I heard the voices within me: *You can do this, Ric.* I can't explain all of this, it was either my mind or something greater in this world; either way, I released all my anger on the world through the best possible way, releasing endorphins and getting fitter. Every time I came in from a run, I would shower and feel so much better, *baby steps* I said to myself. *We have 24 hours in a day, focus on this only, take each hour by hour and one foot in front of the other, nothing else.*

I found for the first few months of losing Jade when I went out running on only two to three hours' sleep, I would have what most medical experts would call a panic attack, just without the brown bag. It was me and the universe and the road, then I would focus on an image of Jade sucking her thumb, an image that brought us back together, the image that made me realise. I knew it would be a journey to pull myself out this black hole I was in. So I decided to just keep running when I could, however long I went. I was facing this head-on through my running and releasing all my anger onto the world within nature. I felt this was the best way of dealing with everything, otherwise I would have pushed many more people away from me, out of anger and the loss of Jade.

When I used to run pre-July 2018, I used to listen to lots of motivational music and parts of the background music really inspired me and gave me adrenaline. So I used to listen to the background music and feel the words being said, but they weren't if you get me, it was like I was saying them to myself, to truly believe I could get through this. So, my running journey started with thinking about every moment when Jade picked me up in bad times throughout my life, at my two redundancy points, for example, and really focused on all the good she did and the amazing life she lived but also realised it was also me that made better choices and put myself in a better place and kept moving forward stronger. This was my focus, and I would share this with the universe within all my energy while running. So, I tried to create positive gravity energy and mindfulness to give me answers and help me, my step one to survival through major milestones in our life, positive images of Jade to try and overcome my current trauma and horrific images that would come to me in the night when I woke or bring me to tears in my sleep, sobbing.

I remember my mum and nana coming to see Hugo in October, and my nana had brought the most beautiful photo frame of what looked like Mary with a baby, but it wasn't if you get me, it looked like Jade and Hugo – grown up around two years. Nana said she had got this from the church and felt it was meant for me, so here it is on my wall in my dining room. My nana is very spiritual and a healing person, so she had the gift, and Jade just loved spending time with my nana, she always said, "I always feel so much better and at peace after 10 minutes with

Nana Guy." Nana always deep down believed I had a gift and always said this to my mum, I think.

Meeting the Hospital

Everyone was training for the 10k run in Leeds for November, and the time had come in October where I had to go and meet the DBTH Hospitals in Doncaster to discuss Jade's case, as a maternal death is extremely rare. About five to seven women pass away due to maternal deaths each year in the UK, and most of this number if not all pass away due to underlying health issues. Jade was fit and healthy, so Jade's case was the only one in the UK, and we needed answers. I went with Jade's mum and Aunty Kim, and we got nothing from the meeting, other than they didn't have any answers, and were just interviewing us for more information. They had done a very inaccurate timeline of events, and some information was given prior to the meeting, but it was a shambles really, and Jade's aunty tore a strip off each one of the directors of the trust, and they didn't have much to say. Their aim was to complete their SI report by November time, and we asked them to commission another trust to challenge what they have done etc. Kim knew what needed doing even more than any of the directors sat around the table, which was very alarming for a non-medic like myself to just look at the leadership team for DBTH; concern came to mind, bigtime. At this point, I feared for all pregnant woman going in to give birth at DBTH.

Hugo was coming up to three months, and I think it was his injections or his first ones, they were not nice, and he screamed the GP down for only a few seconds, which broke me, most things did to be honest. He was still in his basket near my bed at this stage also, but most importantly, we were both in the bedroom, which was key, a little more structure. At this stage, I had given Rocky our cat to Jade's sister Sally who would look after him, but it was too much for me having Hugo and my loss alongside dealing with a fear of cats in the house, what a bloody nightmare. Anyway, off Rocky went, I didn't feel anything really just glad he was out my hair, as I had bigger fish to fry in my life, and needed no extra stress and just simplicity, but I was happy he was going to a good home.

I remember meeting a top friend, Pete, from uni and Jade's family at Farmer Copley's where we had the wake and went for breakfast there and then also went to the Halloween zone outside and got some pumpkins; so crazy to think Hugo was only three or four months old then. It was a lovely day with Pete, Jane and the girls. I remember going home and carving the two pumpkins out; one with mummy on, and the other was a superhero one, the batman sign. It was the time to find some strength to start rising out of this dark hole I was in.

I also arranged a professional photoshoot for Hugo to go to, and he looked adorable, but we were all missing Jade so much, he had so many different outfits on, and I thought I will do everyone frames for Christmas with pro pictures of Hugo in. So that's what I did, and everyone loved them. I have a huge one on my wall above the log burner Jade chose, the photo is me and Hugo with our suits on, and Hugo has his gangster suit and hat on. So cute, she would be so proud.

Jades 10K run in Memory Leeds Abbey Dash

The run came up in November, and we all had t-shirts designed for the race thanks to a friend of Jade's. Everyone turned up for the event, and we must have had 40–50 plus running the race and lots of spectators, so the turnout was out of this world for beautiful Jade. When I set off running, I had my headphones in and decided to listen to the spa music we listened to at birth. Some may be like *are you mad going there*, but my strategy was to go there, deep in amongst all the feelings and darkness and find your own way out, this was one way that helped me massively. Running for Jade, listening to the spa music that reminded me of me massaging her feet, touching her, and her giving birth to Hugo, what a positive focus. As I was running, I felt I was moving forward mentally and physically. All my feelings amongst this unravelled during my run with tears down my eyes and also looking at how far I had come with my strategies and managing with Hugo, but my release of endorphins and feelings just being in the universe took me one step further in my grief. I had done a PB at 48 mins for a 10k, which isn't too bad for me, as I'm more the build for weights and upper body stuff, but got it done for my Pupy, and had so many photos and memories with everyone at the end of the race. I have nothing but pure love for all my family and friends who had supported me so far on my journey with Hugo. Hugo also had his own mummy running t-shirt on and looked so beautiful in his pram.

The run was over, and it had been four months since Jade had passed, and I fell further into a dark place and became very angry with the world and within myself, and also a sense of guilt. There were so many times at the start of my grief, I was thinking *Was this somehow my fault, did Jade die because of me, could I have done something to prevent this in the hospital*? Sounds crazy to most but it's true in terms of what happens. Also, I felt very weak and felt like I needed to see a specialist or counsellor, as I was finding it hard to really vent with anyone around me, and even though family and friends are there to support, which I appreciated, sometimes you need a neutral four-walls chat, about anything, anyone, whatever it may be; vent is the word. I kept on asking for support from the trust, but I was being ignored for a good few weeks, I felt I was being treated like someone who had just lost their wife without the circumstances surrounding Jade's death and also being left with Hugo alone without his mummy and my wife.

I found it hard being around Jade's family - and sometimes my own around six months after Jade or certainly up to Christmas time, not because I didn't appreciate the support they had given me, but we had our own grief journeys going on, with our own anger, denial etc. and thoughts around the loss of Jade. And sometimes it was a lot mentally for me, but I guess it was hard for them around me too, but talking about Jade was key but was just so hard certainly within the first six months for me personally anyway. With Christmas coming up, this was very hard to face. I guess I felt people's heartache and it was very hard to take on, on top of my own and looking after Hugo full time. I deep down thank Jade's family for all their support to me within the first 6–12 months and having Hugo, giving me time to breathe, understand what's happened and take care of my wellbeing, but also them having Hugo I am sure provided valuable therapy and focus for them too.

I guess I am very strong but also very sensitive, which isn't a bad trait at all. I knew though as time would go on, everyone grieving for Jade would come closer together and talk more around losing Jade and our feelings. I guess as I write this now in lockdown, I have faith that this will happen, and anyone grieving for Jade, family/friends and finding it really hard, if you're willing to open up, I'm probably one of the best people to talk to, but I do know all those close to Jade will remain very strong with each other, family/friends etc.

I guess my own journey wasn't helping matters, but for me, life is all about being open. If you're more open, you have more conversations and sharing your journey with those who understood, I guess this is taking steps to healing, which I was miles away from. I guess I was a closed book, so some may have found it hard to really connect with me; only one or two could do this, and I was glad at least it wasn't none. Some may have felt it was hard being around me, but one thing I did know at this stage in my grief, is that 50% of the people in my life could be around me, whether they just sat there with me or not, and the other 50% just disappeared, in terms of contact via text, etc. I get this totally now two years on, everyone is different, and not everyone can connect with someone who has lost like I have. And Jade's loss and my/Hugo's loss was huge so it could have been even harder for most to reach out to me. I guess if people don't know what to say, they don't say anything at all, and just fade away. Which is fine, that's life. Remember the train of life, people get on and off all the time at different stages, but they can also come back, and that's fine.

Thailand – Without Jade Dec 2018

I went away at the end of November to Thailand for 10 nights as I felt I needed to be in touch with all the things and some places me and Jade had been to, and I felt being there at the end was important to me as I saw out 2018. Family supported me looking after Hugo and off I went Bangkok-Krabi-Phi Phi-Krabi-Bangkok. I went with a long-standing friend, although, looking back now, I should have gone on my own, but we live and learn. I'm sure the next time I visit Thailand it will be a completely different experience with a change in feelings.

I ended up back at Railay Beach, which was always a cool spot, then headed for the quiet side of Phi Phi islands, which actually was a great trip and a new experience for me, trekking around the islands and going fishing and cooking our own fish was an experience I will never forget. Visually Thailand was beautiful, but it ended there really, but I know I will be back at the right time and most likely with Hugo creating new memories and I know my feelings will be complete in Thailand. I had this dream recently that I was playing the guitar in Thailand, and Hugo was sat in the wooden bar on the beach listening to his daddy. It was an epic dream; all will be revealed at the end of the book.

I came back home and needed to gear up for Christmas but was dreading the whole thing really, but I felt like I needed to get my shit together. I went to Bawtry Forest where me and Jade would always go and get a Christmas tree and some decs for Hugo to enjoy. The tree looked amazing up, and a few Santa and elf decs, with also some stockings hanging from the fireplace. The only thing was Jade wasn't here with us when she should be. Hugo was only six months at the time, and he was crawling at six months which was mad really, going backwards, but still he wanted to move and go, and I knew he would be strong, like his daddy. I also took Hugo to the Santa's grotto with family where he dressed up as an elf, he didn't really know what was going on, but he did perk up in his eyes when he saw the present, and this brought joy to lots in the family on both sides.

I dreaded the question, which was always the case. As we walked into the grotto, the elf said, "Where's Mummy?" I just ignored it and said let's have the photo done. I didn't want to go into things, and if I don't want to do something, that is exactly what shall happen. I look back at this point, and during the last six months, there were always times where people would look at me and think *Where's mummy?* I guess this was my paranoia, and I had this for a while, other than Portugal and popping out, the rest of the time I was in isolation at home with Hugo, dealing with my grief daily, and fighting hard against this battle of loss, and bringing up Hugo alone. I even remember just going out to the shops, and I was so anxious and felt so nervous with Hugo in his pram, I just felt everyone was looking at me always, but I guess everyone knew about me in the village at this point, so it was hard. I remember hearing two people talk outside the Co-op saying that's that guy who lost his wife at birth, it hit me hard. I knew this would be a journey and my strength would get even more powerful, and I would become more at ease with Hugo socialising out etc. I guess I believed in the healing process also and knew, with time, my heart would heal, or at least patch up.

Christmas day came, and I remember waking up with Hugo and sorting him out and getting him dressed. We went downstairs, opened up some presents, Hugo didn't have a clue really, and headed over to my dad's for 11am for two hours just to say hello, then headed back home for the afternoon as I just wanted to be at home. Jade always wanted Christmas dinner at home when we had Hugo for the first time, so I really wanted to do this in her memory for Jade. New Year came quick, and Jade's family went to Devon and did some special memories for Jade at Beer Beach, marking stones and throwing them in, the videos really hit a string in my heart, but I just wanted to be at home with Hugo, and home started to feel more like home again.

It was the end of the year, and it was the first time me and Jade were not doing our vision boards and refocusing for the year ahead. So, I decided to do Ric's and Hugo's goals. Looking back now at our goals, I smashed most of them, some rolled over into 2020, but Hugo's goals, were:

1. Be good for Daddy
2. Settle sleeping well
3. Say mama for my first word
4. Take my first step at 11 months

I also set some goals for us for 2020 and one that stood out for me, which was hilarious, was "stop pulling hair and head-butting kids" (we're getting there, lol).

Remember this was a projection as Hugo was only six months old. I'm a huge believer in writing a goal down and looking at it weekly, as subconsciously you work harder to get it done, and this worked for me. Well, everything I wrote down for Hugo came true, he did walk at 11 months, and he did say mama for his first word, and he sleeps so well, 8pm-6am flat out. I felt we needed another run in memory of Jade and maybe something new for everyone to work towards, so I stepped up the pace and entered Retford half-marathon for March 2019. Loads of friends and family again entered with me, and the New Year started with a focus and some form of purpose. So, looking back at 2018 these were what allowed me to drop my feet onto the bedroom floor each morning moving into 2019:

1. I had believed many messages had come through from the spirit world from Jade, to find the light.
2. Being in touch with the universe through my training, and releasing my anxiety in the best possible way doing 10-20km + runs.
3. Finding a smile within me over time, being with Hugo and believing in a greater force.
4. Gratitude at all levels, even just breathing and finding a way to be in the present, without worrying about the future. I believe in the domino effect of thoughts and choices, and I want my future self to look back and thank me for all I did and decisions I made.

Just to end 2018, I remember one night in December. I was asleep, and Hugo was next to me, and I woke up in the middle of the night, and there were three people stood around my bed. I said out loud, "I know you're there, Jade, with others, I can see you." I wasn't scared, but when I woke the next morning, I was like *Jesus, what was that around my bed last night?*

2019 prevails. My first year without Jade

Hugo started nursery in January for two half days, giving me eight hours a week to try and relax, recharge etc., but I used this time to run, swim, cycle. I thought if I train harder and get fitter, then I will sleep better and at some point, my body will thank me. I had Retford half-marathon in my sight, so this was a great focus for me. I was so glad Hugo went to nursery as he was a quick mover, crawling at six months and he was also being weaned by the nursery, which was a massive help for me anyway. I always remember when turning up at the nursery, nobody asked at first, but I bet they were thinking *Where's mummy?* I didn't tell them at the start but was intending to at my own pace, but Jade's mum informed them, I think, when she went to pick Hugo up one Tuesday, so that was that, which was fine. I always felt empty turning up at nursery every week, seeing mums and dads getting out their cars and walking their kids into nursery. I guess the staff would have felt my anxiety as I would just drop him off and pick him up. I did find common ground with one of the staff. She was lovely, as she used to be a runner, and I would turn up in my running gear. Every time Hugo was dropped off at 9am, I would then run 20km, have a shower, coffee, have 20 minutes to myself then start planning on picking him up for 1pm. At the start, my body was battered, and my inner strength and power allowed me to run so far on only 3–4 hours' sleep per night, as I was still waking with nightmares and sobbing in my sleep waking myself up, with a wet face due to tears, waking just thinking *Where are you, Jade?* I remember also when I ran for miles while Hugo was at nursery, I would listen to all the motion music that always was in the background of most motivational talks/music. This allowed me to think about all the times I picked myself back up in my life, and all the times I would listen to motivational music from 2016 onwards. But now it was just me and the background music, and I started to say the words myself, instead of someone else or me listening to somebody else. This was transformational for me and proved to be over time. One song actually being called 'Time' by Hans Zimmer.

I also had a log cabin weekend away with Jade's family in January, which Jade organised I think for her mum's birthday, so I decided to go. It was a chilled weekend away actually; there was a hot tub that Hugo loved, and I remember telling Jade's family about our story when I came back for her, and she said she was engaged to someone else. It is a funny story with so much meaning. The Sunday dinner was amazing in the village, and we went to a local town for a meal and drinks one day. My dad's party was also end of January although his birthday was early January, this was certainly something to look forward to. Six months had passed, and I was still in this dark hole, with a skinhead as I shaved my head in Bangkok, I felt I needed a new look, as I felt I wasn't me all round, so why look like me. Dad's party came round so quickly, and we had the party in his kitchen with a singer also. Everyone got pretty hammered, and I had a few beers. I remember my bro Neil had been to China and got this spirit, it was horrible. Myself and Jade's friend Louise had a moment together over Jade, as she was being missed, and I guess it hits people harder at different times. All my bros and sister slept at my house. I woke up the next morning with a hangover, which I was so happy about; my body was doing normal things. As before, it wouldn't touch the sides, but saying that I don't get hangovers, but it was all worth it.

Jade Laid to Rest

Behind the scenes, I had chosen the perfect headstone and body piece for Jade, and chose perfect photos for us, and the wording and design was exactly how I wanted it. I requested for the stone to be laid on 14 February 2019, which meant the world to me, and the memorial business did this. I remember waking up on the morning, and knew it was being laid around 10–11am. All the family knew this was the case, so I knew her resting place would have been busy that day. The grave is like a Jade green feel all over, with Jade stones in the middle. On the grave it says, *'I've loved you for a thousand years'*, from me and *'I will go wherever you will go'* from Hugo. There is also a picture of me and Jade on the stone, which looks like I've passed away but it's what I wanted. I guess if I passed away, I would want to be laid with Jade and my headstone facing hers directly. When I turned up to see Jade, there were many family members there, but they all left to give me space, which I respected, and so did they. I felt this was the day I started to turn a corner slightly even though it had been eight months-ish. I felt I had laid her to rest properly as before we had a cross for her, which was a lovely idea by Jade's aunty, and I would change the funeral florist flower piece that said 'Pupy' every two weeks due to the flowers dying. Jade's sister would sometimes come down and help me, which I appreciated. I think I sometimes did a better job than the bloody florist (joke) and have a photo of the flower changes in a frame in my front room, as this meant the world to me and was helping my soul heal, I suppose, without me even realising it at the time. I remember driving away from Jade that day and away from the cemetery, smiling and crying at the same time, as I knew I had done a beautiful thing for Jade and loved doing this.

End of February 2019 was a mad one, as I went to my mate's stag do in Lisbon, and I wasn't really in the best of places. All my buddies knew I wasn't there fully, but I was glad I was just sat with close friends having a beer away from home, which gave me the time I needed. On my arrival back home, I went and ran 10k with my brothers, as my brother Neil is CEO of Burnley FC, he was helping promote the Burnley runner who ran to every away game all season, which is bloody crazy. He ran from Burnley to Newcastle, but we organised to meet him 10k from the stadium and run in with him and watch the Burnley-Newcastle game. This was an experience to see and also spend time with my brothers, and I guess also it was a warmup before Retford half-marathon.

Retford Half-Marathon 2019

Every time I had a planned trip away, something major would always surface regarding Jade dying just before I went away, and I had my brother's stag do in Las Vegas coming up in March and also the Retford half-marathon before that. I focused on my running journey and all that it had done for me so far, and how it made me feel when I ran and all the positive things I focused on and images in my head, so I focused on this for the Retford run. My aim was to think about all the pain and suffering Jade, me and Hugo have had up to this stage, and released all this when running, and this is exactly what happened. Although I was ill for the run, I still managed to run it and complete it in 2.02hrs, which I was pleased about under the circumstances and also being ill. You couldn't wear headphones for this one, and I felt I was lost without my music, but got through it, within my own thoughts and battles in my head. The turnout for the run was amazing, and I think lots surprised themselves, remembering also this was not 10k this was 21k. A massive round of applause to all my friends and family who did this and believed before they couldn't. Nice to say, guys, (I ran a half-marathon) all for Jade.

I wasn't done there, I had always had a visual in my head that I would run a full marathon and Jade be at the finishing line with Hugo in her arms, had this even before July 2018. Me and Jade spoke about this a lot, and after the birth we said, I would choose a course and do it nine months after Jade had given birth, meaning I would put my body through hard work and pain for nine months, and do the run at the end just like Jade had done nine months with Hugo in her belly and gave birth. She said, "Deal." This is true love; this is massive respect for each other and why we had a love like no other.

Las Vegas March 2019

It was time for Vegas, so off I went for Gatwick, I parked up went over to the Premier Inn, and met my brother and all his friends ready for the trip. Hugo was being looked after by family, which I was so grateful for. I flew on my own with Norwegian as I booked late on. The flight was great, although they swindled you on the food and drink purchases, but the flight was great and the service. I arrived and dived into a taxi heading for the Excalibur where all the lads were. All my brothers were there also, which was good for me, as Andy's friends are top lads and defo know how to drink. But I guess I was still not in the best of places, and was very much in my anger stage, as lots was happening in the background regarding Jade passing, and guilt was right back in my face, thinking, *What could I have done in the hospital to prevent this? How could I have stopped Jade from dying?* I guess I had to accept this wasn't my fault, the responsibility sat with the hospital.

I decided to drink heavily each day for seven days and just get smashed and try to just park my life and all that was going on. I had some great memories and loved a good gamble, so Vegas is definitely my place. The break was what I needed, and it's always amazing to spend time with my brothers and his friends, gambling drinking and partying. I won a few but also lost a few, that's the game, but it was fun. I will never forget the night my brother Andy got smashed down near the link, and his best man and my other brother had to take him home, that video will live on. As I flew to Vegas on my own, I also flew back, and remember on my way home, actually ready to come home, due to drinking too much but was dreading what was to come to be honest. I was sorting out lots within the home behind closed doors alongside looking after Hugo and awaiting the inquest and further reports regarding Jade, alongside a few weddings coming up. Just turning up for events was a massive step for me, period, as my head was still a fucking mess.

When I arrived back home, I organised and put in place my counsellor, who was only 10 minutes down the road from me, so we started to have sessions every other week. At the time, this really helped, as anger and guilt together was not a good combination at this point, so I would just vent about anything, anyone to my counsellor. At the start, it was me talking 90% of the time as I guess she didn't have a circumstance like mine. The one thing I took from my sessions going forward was not to worry about the future and also don't take too much on and gain the strength to put things down, coming back to it, and put things down for good. My focus was Hugo and my health, and I really focused on this from April 2019 onwards, and I know this will always be my focus going forward; health is wealth.

My good friend Pete Taylor, AKA Pedro, after Retford half-marathon took the bold decision to run a full marathon in Manchester, and due to me being in Vegas this stalled me doing this, but mentally I wasn't there or ready for it. But I'm so glad Pete did this for him, more importantly, and for many other reasons that pushed him to do this, but this was the inspiration and push I needed. After Pete completed his marathon, that evening I opened the laptop and took major action and entered the Yorkshire Marathon in October, intending to do what I always wanted to do for Jade, run a marathon. The only issue is inside I was saying sorry to Jade for not running it in April, which was the 9-month mark and also my intention all along. But I realised I needed to cut myself some slack and October worked better for me but still nine months training in 2019 up to October. So that was that my training started in terms of picking up my distance, but I realised I only had one day a week to do long runs as Hugo went to his grandparents on a Tuesday and Tuesday night, but this was my window to do long distance. I thank Pedro massively for indirectly giving me the nudge I needed. Personally, I thought, well the longer I run, the more time I have to think about me and Jade, what had happened, where I was in the present and my small goals going forward, but embracing the challenge for Jade but also my sanity and mental state. Also, I thank my two uni pals Pedro and Alcock massively for the first six months after Jade more so, the things they were doing for me really kept me going. So, boys, much love to you guys for this bigtime.

A couple of months flew by, and my brother had his wedding, which was a truly beautiful day and to spend time with all the family was lovely. The barn house was amazing alongside a great wedding scene, day and evening do. The breakfast in the morning was one of my best experiences I have had, as the setting was perfect. My friend Ash from university also got married, and this was also another amazing bash, but I guess when you're with friends it felt different, and I still wasn't myself, which was fine, but I didn't feel like dancing or socialising much; also, I wasn't very well so this didn't help. But again, I found the strength to be there, and I'm sure Ash appreciated my presence, so I left early that night. Ash and I go way back with university, but we grew closer as friends after university, and he came to Thailand and was one of my best men at my wedding, which I'm truly grateful for.

Spring was ending, and I looked back at all I had achieved so far, and how much more I was getting out socialising and being with Hugo outdoors. I just always said when times were really hard, and I would sob into my heart for Jade, I just heard the words *You've got this, you're strong, Hugo needs you.* I hope one day, Hugo grows up to see all his daddy did in memory of Mummy, and he sees me as his inspiration, his idol. This is my major goal in life.

The running wasn't really happening, but I believed I could run 20k no problem without any pulls or puffs, so I placed faith in me to start when the time was right. I was keeping busy actively, which was my medicine as I wasn't turning to the bottle, drugs, or anything that I knew would create or give me a huge setback based on my current state. The one thing I knew was a massive milestone as I wasn't thinking of death anymore looking at Hugo, and I wasn't having any more suicidal thoughts, as they would be in my mind daily for months during the second half of 2018. This was huge, and I had certainly pulled myself up from the black hole, and there was a glimmer of light.

Another break came up, which was a holiday in Cyprus and was Hugo's first holiday. I loved that I had also set up an Insta page @hugoandricstravels so this was my picture drop not only for all to see, but also Hugo to take over one day when he gets a lot older. I went with Jade's family, and it was a lovely break away, and I'm sure they were blessed to experience Hugo's first holiday away with him. I guess Jade's family were also having their own grief journey so being with Hugo for his first holiday helped them, I'm sure. I remember towards the end of the holiday, I went on a jet ski and whizzed across the water one morning, it was so flat and clear the water, but I felt free, I was out to sea, in the sun, thinking of Jade always but knew I was getting stronger in myself. I had mastered the silence though, from Jade passing up to May 2019, all the times I wanted to shout, scream, put my fist through a door, I didn't, I found calmness and silence, which was huge for me.

Two days after Cyprus, I decided with a friend to cycle from my pal Ben's house (Thorne, Doncaster) to the Lake District, this was a pretty crazy and a great trek on our bikes, but this is what I needed at nearly the year point since Jade, so I was so thankful of Ben for organising most of it. We did pretty damn well, we got to Bradford day one, where we hit a two-mile uphill road in Bradford, I called it the kiss of death to myself. Day two we then headed into the Lakes via Leeds. And it was beautiful, especially when we hit Skipton. My legs were smashed to pieces, and I can't explain the pain I experienced on arrival, my pal was so happy, but I was hanging out my arse and needed a minute to just stop and think. Six ice baths did the job, and I felt OK the next day. Ben had organised for us to go canyoning, which was my first experience and so cool. Canyoning for those who don't know is swimming down waterfalls and going down ropes and jumping off small cliffs into the water. This is just what I needed, to be in touch with nature, but also what an achievement to cycle to the Lakes; I think it was about 120 miles. All this long-distance exercise was doing me wonders in terms of my mental state and also my self-belief. Self-belief and confidence is everything, without this, you are worthless to yourself and others, and with it, the world is there for you to challenge and enjoy all it has to offer. Me and Jade always believed the biggest currency was influencing others positively, there's nothing more powerful for me.

July 2019 had come around quick, and I was getting my smart attire on as I needed to head for the courts in Nottingham for Jade's inquest, the pain and my anxiety was through the roof, trust me, although the inquest had changed to a pre-inquest due to further information etc. Myself, Jade's mum and Aunty Kim came with me, and I am grateful for all the support they had shown. As we arrived at the courts, we got called up to be informed that the pre-inquest was due to the matter being passed to our Law enforcement Officers for a much more serious set of investigations. I felt so mad and sad and angry inside all at once, as I felt my stomach had been ripped out again, but all that was on my mind was staying strong. Like I say, it's always bad news or new information that hits when an event is like two days away, and Hugo's first birthday was days away, so I needed to organise and ensure this went to plan. As mentioned later in the book, my focus writing this book is not around how and why Jade died, this book is about love, passion, resilience and hope and our lives together. The four very corners that I know will create a strong life for me and Hugo going forward.

Hugo's first birthday hit, and I invited all friends and family, it was at the Pantry where we had Jade's birthday celebration after she had passed away. I suppose Hugo's birthday will always be hard due to the circumstances. We had an amazing Peter Rabbit cake and cupcakes for Hugo, and I did a spread for everyone. It was just great to bring everyone back together, but the day felt hard, I think it always will, but I know my heart will heal as years go on, all heals, I guess the pain remains, but strength prevails. Hugo was taking steps by then and could stand up, so he was wobbling around everyone, and it was a great first birthday for him. He's such a special, beautiful boy, and I can't wait to share all my adventures with him. We also had Leeds 10k in memory of Jade again the day after so this was a busy week and weekend. I was always focused on having foresight and looking towards hard times maybe and ensuring something good prevailed, and the run was definitely a good thing for everyone on such a happy and sad weekend without Jade and with Hugo.

I always remember my pal Ash arriving for the run and also Uncle Andy, who were new to the running group for Jade, which is so great to see. Although Ash broke his ankle doing it, always bloody Ash, hilarious. This time around, I got my medal engraved in memory of Jade, we had so many more photos and headed for the pub afterwards. My time wasn't as fast this time around but, my training wasn't for speed, as I was gearing up for my marathon for October. But realised quite quickly, I hadn't done much training, and had only three months till the race, running once a week, but I just believed it would happen, my inner strength would take me. I hadn't mentioned this at this stage, but I had a few tattoos in memory of Jade, and some may have thought "A bloody tattoo", but I didn't care what people thought, it was about why I was doing it and my feelings around it, I had waited for a year to mull on the idea, and I still wanted them. So that's what I did, I had Hugo on one arm in Thai writing with a green love heart below it, so saying his full name Hugo Hart but in Thai and with a symbol, and I did the same for Jade on the other wrist. But I had writing going up my arm too, "I will go wherever you will go" the Calling song as this is on the grave too. And also on Jade's part, "I have loved you for a thousand years" which is also on the grave and our two songs. I think it looks great, makes me feels good, looking at them daily, and it's something that stays with me forever in memory of a true angel.

A week later I went off to Benidorm for four days with Pedro, my good friend, which was a weekend much needed. I had so much going on later in spring and early summer with Jade's case, Hugo's development, and keeping busy was key alongside my grief journey. All I needed was to talk to a great friend and have beers and try to enjoy life again, and I got this on my trip. I believe it's not where you are sometimes, its who you're with. The last full day was epic, we got bikes and cycled the whole coast, hit bar after bar, we got to pint 15, I think, by 5.30pm then realised we need to get the bikes back for 6pm otherwise I would have been charged £300. We made it, headed back home, got changed and went out for our final evening. I walked past a tattoo shop and said to Pete, "Let's do this." In we went, Pete was brave as it was his first tattoo, so I got RJH in italic at the top of my neck on my back, as my name is Richard James Hart, but it also it stood for Ric, Jade, Hugo, how mad is that. Pedro had a dragonfly on his back with some colour in, it was epic, funny, and a moment to remember. "Café Benidorm it had been emotional", and we headed home. I was very proud of how far I had come, to find a way to relax laugh and have a little fun again.

My aim for 2019 was to stay active and doing adventure type things with good people where I could connect with them and also the universe, and I had done this. The cycle trip with Ben, my holiday with Pedro, Las Vegas with my brothers, and also Cyprus with Jade's family and my family in Spain. Me and Jade always went on holidays, and I certainly was not stopping this in my life. I really connected with Pedro in Benidorm and I knew I would, he's that kind of guy, a true legend. It was just the trip I needed, and when I came home and had collected Hugo and gone to bed that night, I remember sitting up out of bed, and thinking about seeing Jade pass away in the hospital, seeing her in the funeral directors, and it was the first time I didn't fall and break to my knees, all I saw was her sucking her thumb, smiling at me with that grin we all know of. And this happening, I knew, something positive was happening with my thoughts, and I had taken a major step forward in my mind to find peace, and I was self-healing but also doing something very clever in my mind.

I also remember going for a run after Benidorm as this was my training zone now for the Yorkshire Marathon and I had three months till the race. I found a lane near me which was a 5km straight country lane, so I was running back and forth on this, and it started off hard work, as my car was nearby and going back and forth, and knowing you have to go again and again, is even harder than just doing a large loop, honest. I had Jade in my mind always, all our special memories, the strength I had gained over the last few months, and really felt another gravity of energy with the universe as I ran, with pure self-belief that I would complete 42km for Jade, as I felt this would be my final push or big achievement for 2019. So I gave it my all, with only training for one day a week-ish (long-distance anyway). I wanted to show for myself and to everyone around me it can be done, even with limited time, it can be done.

Jade's birthday came around again, and she would have been 35 this year, and it was spent driving to Helmsley where we went together back in August 2017. I remember it so clearly; we went around the town, walked around all the quirky shops, vintage and charity, as Jade just loved a good charity shop, and then we headed for the large green house where we went for food and gin. Then we headed to a Michelin star restaurant nearby. So, we did this again, but with Jade's family, then we headed for a spa there, which was lovely. Me and Jade just loved a spa, get our slippers and robes on and we were set. Jade just loved how in touch I was with my feminine side. Another reason why we clicked and kept on clicking. Me and Hugo headed for the grave where we laid flowers and cards on mummy's grave, and I said, "Mummy will go wherever you will go to, Hugo." He just looked at me and pointed at Mummy. This snapped me in half, I was just thinking, *How do I get through the big step which is going through the journey of telling Hugo about his mummy and all that comes with it?* But I didn't want to worry, and stayed strong and thought, *Go with your gut, Ric, end of.* Things will work out pretty OK doing this, and I believed I would be in a better place telling the story of Mummy and Daddy to Hugo. I knew two onwards was the journey around this.

Me and Hugo had another holiday to look forward to in September, and this was at my dad's new pad in Spain. He had bought a great place on a complex with its own private pools, and wow, the place was great. Location was even better, as it was in Moreira, and close to so much in Spain on the south-east coast. So anyway rewind, it was my first time taking Hugo on holiday on a plane. I remember pulling up to East Midlands and getting out, with a bag and Hugo's bag around my shoulders each way, my right hand was pulling the large case, my left hand had Hugo's car seat under my arm, and my left hand was pushing his buggy. Stressed wasn't the word, trust me. I certainly got some looks, either girls thought I was good-looking, or they thought *Jesus, what's going on there?* More than likely the latter, it looked like I was emigrating.

I got to the gate for them to tell me there are delays and Hugo was getting restless, so I just pushed him around departure for like an hour, checked in the car seat and case, and I felt free going through duty-free. When I got onto the plane, I left the buggy at the bottom of the stairs as you do, but I remember as I was sat down with Hugo, looking out the window, there was a man trying to dismantle my pram. I had forgotten to dismantle it, and he looked really mad, it was quite a funny moment, actually, as a woman had to come over and sort it out for him, I was glad as I bloody needed that. I sat next to an old lady who was travelling with a group, she started chatting to me, and we got on, always good to connect with someone on a plane. I was dreading it, the question, and it came, "So where's Mummy, is she meeting you out there…?" I paused for two seconds and thought *I'm stronger now and have to be strong enough to talk about it*, so I told her she had passed away, and I'm a full-time daddy. Well, she nearly fell to her knees in tears, she kept on saying sorry, I just reassured her she wasn't meant to know, and we carried on talking. I remember as we landed in Spain, I got out with Hugo and the plane was a shitty Ryanair box plane, and I got a round of applause from like 10 people behind me, people saying "great job, mate". It must have been the woman's group she was in and had told them.

The holiday was great, and nice to spend some time with Dad and Liz, and for them to see Hugo more. Being out in Spain made me think about a holiday home for me and Hugo one day, Moreira town was really nice and quirky, we were always busy every day out and about. One day we did the markets, which was great, I bought a new Joey from *Friends* bag, lol, and some lovely things for Hugo. I remember standing in the town with Hugo and sat in front of me was Sam Allardyce, the old England boss. My dad told me he lived there, as it was quite an affluent area defo. My favourite day was Calpi beach, it was great as Hugo loved the waves, and also building sandcastles. I was pleased that I had got to travel lots in 2019 so far, Las Vegas, Lisbon, Cyprus, Spain, and got to share new holidays with Hugo. Cyprus and Spain weren't bad for his first year with Daddy, I knew Hugo would grow to be a brown boy like his Mummy and Daddy. One day I know I will get a holiday home for me and Hugo and can't wait to choose which country becomes our second home. Sun, sea and sand come to mind. (Hugo's Villa.)

My marathon crept up so quickly but looking back from August and September. I managed to do long runs every Tuesday, then rest Tuesday evening, as Hugo was at Jade's family. I am sure Jade's family were pleased to have Hugo lots, but I was also mindful of how much he was around Jade's and my family, and due to my family still working etc., it was harder for my mum and dad and brothers and sisters to be around Hugo as much as they wanted to. But I know they will be in Hugo's life more and more as he grows, and they will experience what Jade's family had with Hugo early days. It's all about balance, but most importantly it's about Hugo having a strong relationship with all his family tree (I'm sure he will have his favourites). I guess he will be shared across many on weekends going forward but also if he stays at home for the weekend, being with his daddy, going out, that's what shall happen. Life will find some form of normality, and I guess me and Hugo will live a busy life when he's 3–4 years old, which I'm so looking forward to. Anyway, back to my running, I started at 12k running for July and built up to 29k up to the beginning of October, which is bloody amazing only being able to do one big run a week. On that straight lane near me, with my music in and my thoughts, I guess I just got stronger and stronger over the summer, and certain parts of the motivation music didn't break me like it used to, so I knew I was healing inside, or just getting stronger and more resilient. As I ran for 25k each week, I thought about all Jade's life with me, and all she had achieved, and that smile while sucking her thumb, and her laugh, and what we had, and I felt pure gratitude of love and felt blessed with what I had with Jade, with still tears coming down my face, but gratitude tears, not lost dark tears.

The day came, and it was marathon day, I remember it all so well. I had only about four hours sleep the night before just due to thoughts etc. in my head, which didn't help at all. My brother Andy was doing the 10-miler, so it was great we went together for this. When I woke that morning, I was grateful for each day waking and seeing Hugo and thought lots about what Jade had missed but felt strong and good about all that I had achieved with Hugo and how far I had come to this point. Now 42km may seem a lot to most, bearing in mind I had only trained once a week, long-distance, but everything is all in your mind, trust me. During the run, I disappeared totally in my head and just thought about the 15–16 years we had together as I ran. I completed it in 4 hours and 50 minutes, although I was on for around 4 hours 25 mins, but just fell apart at the end. But I didn't stop, I kept on going, moving and pushing on for Jade; remember, I had only trained up to 29km.

Also, I did this all on my own, so this could have seemed harder for most, I didn't need an audience for this one. I crossed the finishing line as I intended, and that was the moment I believed in myself and the journey I had come on without Jade and also how far I had come with Hugo. I was proud of myself for the first time properly and couldn't believe I had run a marathon. Running for 4 hrs 50 minutes, thinking about 16 years, helped me not even think about my legs or the pain. It goes to show the mind is powerful, so be wise in terms of what you think and what you believe in. The next day I went swimming and had no pain, I was amazed and so was my brother, I believe this was down to my mind not focusing on running. I'm sure we have all had moments where we are running or cycling and talking to a friend and not focusing on what we are doing, then you look up and go wow look how much we have done, that's your mind. Focus on positive people, focus on inspiring, focus on doing good in this world, focus on challenging yourself positively, and you will win in life.

I remember sitting down at home the next day after my run, and I had my medal on round my neck, sat in my chair, feeling quite low like it had all come to an end, my focus and goals. But did it bollox, I thought to myself, *I have a life to live with my boy, and I'm going to ensure we both live the best possible life going forward as we deserve this bigtime, we deserve peace and happiness at all angles.* I had also thought about my strength and also the amazing memories me and Jade shared and created. We all live and die, some live on till 80-plus some don't, but one thing is for sure, I'm sure anyone can gather that Jade lived life to the full, always on the edge of the cliff, didn't care about tomorrow and lived for today, and what she did and what we did in our lifetime most wouldn't achieve in theirs even up to 60–70. We travelled the world, spent money freely without a worry, had a very unique love and bond, and being soulmates and having each other was a weight in gold itself. I was truly blessed to have 15–16 years of my life with Jade. But still to this day I think, *Was Jade meant to die, was this fate?* Well, let me run this by you, go back to the start of the book, if I hadn't had gone out on that night out, would Jade still be alive today? I can't think like that anyway; otherwise guilt will destroy me forever, but do you believe in fate??

- My last-minute choice to get on that minibus to Wakefield back in 2002.
- Jade making friends in Birmingham with my cousin's pal, there's lots of humans in Birmingham but it had to be him, that brought us back in touch.
- The photo I saw of Jade and my decision to get her back after she went travelling.
- Our engagement party at Hugo's house in Crystal Bar in 2013, this bar could have been called anything, but was Hugo's.
- Living our Thailand Dream.
- Travelling the world on many holidays during 2015–2018; about 20 destination holidays.
- Jade's pregnancy journey – 12-week scan on my birthday, 20-week scan Valentine's Day, 30-week 4D scan on our anniversary date. What are the odds? This was fate, meant to be, you can't create this, and the odds are stupid.
- Our baby boy Hugo.
- His heart-shaped birthmark as our surname is HART.
- The spiritual thing happening in my house and with me. (Also, lately a handprint appeared on the window facing Hugo's playpen, where Jade's tree of life is, and it had her handprint. It's the exact same size as this is, the same as the 3D one I had done when she was at the funeral director's).
- The time stopping at 10.09 and 5.00 on her favourite clocks in the house.

Just for a minute, stack all this up, leading up to Jade passing. It just completely baffles my head, to be honest. I was meant to go self-employed and work like 10 hours a week and spend the rest of my time enjoying Jade's pregnancy and being with her each day. I suppose we all have our own theories, but I have my own beliefs anyway. But to be honest, I go back and forth with this as fate and not fate, and I suppose it's an ongoing battle, and something I will have to live with forever really, a lifetime sentence, but one thing I do know is I will put it down and let it go.

My running journey didn't stop there. I had Doncaster 10k left to do in November, the turnout wasn't as big as Leeds, but I knew the runs would slow down over time, and I was fine with this. My aim is to ensure I was getting through my journey the best possible way at the hardest points, and Hugo was developing well.

2019 came to a close, Christmas day was harder than 2018, to be honest, and I fell ill due to this over two or three days, but I bounced back. But typing this now, I'm in a totally different place and can't wait to enjoy Dec 2020 with my boy and whoever else is around us if anyone due to the pandemic. Who knows as rules change every week due to COVID 19 and the outbreak? But I know I'm ready to celebrate life again and Christmas with my boy.

I look back to the dark hole I was in on the floor with no strength to climb back up. But I found a way to see the light, I found a way to turn negative trauma into positivity and future focus through self-belief and my own inner strength/strategies and drive to keep Jade's memory alive, putting all my anxiety and depression into my running, and turning dark, negative thoughts into positive memories of Jade's life.

Jade, I made you proud, and your value and life will always live on within me and Hugo. A truly special girl who will never be forgotten. This book is my legacy to Jade, which will live on for decades through my family tree, and Jade will never be forgotten. Hugo's kids' kids will read this one day, which is just crazy to think about when Hugo will be at the helm.

Pandemic 2020 – Lockdown COVID 19

As we all know COVID 19 hit the world early 2020 and lockdown was official around 18th March in England and I was faced with what could have been my biggest challenge, and certainly was one of them. As the world was also experiencing a sense of grief with a certain level of loss, I felt the world had become parallel to my world just slightly, and all I had gone through in terms of loss and isolation from July 2018 to December 2018. I remember at the start of lockdown all my anxiety and worry came back as I thought *shit, no more nursery, no more childminder to support with Hugo during the week, no Friday nights free*, which was like half the week he was away busy, giving me time to breathe, dealing with what had happened, and keeping fit and busy within myself and my mind and also socialising and keeping on top of the house and my life, and keeping my health at the forefront of everything. I also had Jade's case, which was still pending investigations via Public Services and other regulatory bodies overseeing the NHS, which was not helping, but I ensured I kept it together, and I know in time the truth will come out, it always does. And justice will prevail for Jade, and me and Jade's family will keep pushing where needed.

The first few days were pure meltdown for me in lockdown, but I sat down that evening two days into lockdown, and it felt like my journey had started again from July 2018, being isolated with Hugo and all the similar feelings resurfacing. But I stopped and thought and focused on all of my achievements and knew this was again fate, part of my journey with Hugo. I just loved time with him every day, watching him grow and our routine got even better. I reflected on all the charity runs I organised in memory of Jade, all the pain I let go of into nature while running, how far Hugo had come in his development and growth. I also added up on my phone the total km I had run since July 2018 up to lockdown, and it came to about 1000km. An exchange for loving you, Jade, for a thousand years. At this point, the light bulb came on, it was time to follow my ideas and thoughts and turn this into action, so I decided to create poetry and write.

During lockdown when the world/nature was healing due to everyone staying in their house, so was my heart and soul, deep down, I suppose, or certainly starting to. Of course, I have had challenging times during lockdown, but my focus was day by day and enjoying the outdoors with my boy and watching him blossom. I also would take Hugo out for drives every day and drive the routes that I had run over the last 12–18 months, to help battle with the loss of Jade and my mental state. Most days I would drive out and just be sobbing in my car, with losing Jade, but also thinking about how much I had done, and how far I had come, that's on the running front and my inner strength. I remember driving on the marathon lane I trained on, and I got out the car one evening with Hugo asleep, and looked upon it and thought, *you were my worst enemy but also my best friend*, as silly as it sounds, that lane saved me. And looking back now after driving down this lane up and down, I say to myself *Go on, brother, you did six laps of this for fun on so many occasions, about 30km. Wow, what a dark place I must have been in.*

I decided to be creative in lockdown and think outside the box and turn my lockdown experience into a truly positive one. I achieved the below while looking after a 21-month-old baby full time, which most would say bloody hell, but I just found structure and focus, and was up at 5am each day and made the most of 24 hours in a day. As I always say, there is always time, you just have to make it and want to do it for a reason that fuels your heart and soul.

I designed and created a bedtime story book for Hugo called *Hugo and Daddy's Night-time Adventures,* which has turned into a huge success and was published 12 October 2020 and available on Amazon and other major online distributors. All the proceeds of the book are going to Cruse Bereavement Care Charity. The creation of the book turned negative trauma into positive magic in the sky for Hugo when I read this book to him at night.

I am writing the end of the book now as we speak, which is a huge achievement but helped me in so many ways. Hugo will now have something tangible that will live on forever through his family and their family, and Jade will never be forgotten in years to come. Jade also lives on within the book, so people who want Jade's book will have access to her, based on her life with me through my eyes.

I ran the distance to Nottingham and Sheffield on the spot in my front room to keep fit.

I raised £500 for the NHS in this horrible pandemic to give something back to the world through running and getting people involved and decided to send the money to Captain Tom Moore, who raised over £30million on his conquest to do 100 laps of his garden before his 100th birthday.

And this one is pretty cool, I think. I taught myself to play the guitar, as I had a dream in lockdown which was of me in Thailand with Hugo playing the guitar, and it looked and felt so real, so I bought a guitar the next day, looked at some YouTube videos and self-taught.

The two songs I can now play are the Calling 'Wherever You Will Go' and also Christina Perri 'Thousand Years' – not perfect but playing them within a few weeks of self-teach is bloody amazing, and I'm so proud I did this, and it was great therapy for me too. Not forgetting these are our two songs and are embedded on Jade's headstone. Hugo again will look back at his page and go, "Wow, Daddy did that." Well, I hope so, he already is trying to play my guitars.

I also designed a new garden, creating peace and relaxation, which is and will always be at the top of my agenda in life going forward, giving it a spa feel with a hot tub, firepit, pizza oven and loungers.

My final project when lockdown eased around June was when I created a website in memory of Jade, which brings Jade and our story together. www.jadehartpupylove.co.uk and also a YouTube page which is jadehartpupylove. The main aim of this was to bring people together and share and learn more about Jade through images and people's memory of their images.

The children's book for Hugo and my book of our life together has turned negative trauma during lockdown into seeing some form of light for Jade and allows her to live on within the books in such a beautiful way. It also turns negative trauma into positive magic and memory for Hugo, and has certainly lit up my heart inside, meaning this has contributed towards my healing process and my ongoing grief journey for Jade 100%. I also believe I'm focusing on positivity and hope, through my book creations, channelling energy into these beautiful projects, that not only have helped me but may just help someone else who is going through grief.

In summary, I didn't have my fitness/running to turn to as my distraction for the loss of Jade, so writing *Pupy Love*, learning the guitar and doing Hugo's children's book sparked the fire inside. Everyone will find their own way in grief, and some stay stuck within it (Denial Anger Depression), but I found my place to deal with everything emotionally. I did it, and I am an enormously proud dad. As I write this now, lockdown is easing, and the world is switching back on where pubs, restaurants, cinemas etc. are reopening so people can come together again to find some form of normality on 4 July and going forward.

Having been out and about during post-lockdown, the world is not the same again, and I think won't be for a good three years yet, to be honest. Lockdowns, precautions and movement around the world are going to be a 5-year back and forth problem, in my opinion. It's also been interesting speaking to lots around me in terms of their own opinions of the pandemic and rulings around this and their own current circumstances. Quite frankly, we are all grieving in some shape or form, grieving the loss of free movement, the impact it has had on them financially, the impact it has had on their household and also themselves and also their mental health, some may have lost loved ones due to COVID 19.

Regarding the pandemic, some were at denial stage, some are angry, some are totally depressed, but finding the strength to say to yourself, "Hey, I'm alive, my feet can touch the ground as I wake, and I have air in my lungs for me to have faith that each day may get better, and maybe find inspiration to get new hobbies or manage mindsets," is exactly how we need to think. Be creative people and appreciate the fact you have your family/loved ones around you. Lockdown, in summary, made me a stronger person, it made me face up to so much in terms of losing Jade but also gave me inspiration to refuel the fire in my soul to believe life has to go on, and I am going to make it as good as it can be for me and Hugo. We only get one life so, my god, I'm going to live it when I can.

This is also a full circle of experience from 4 July 2018 to July 4 July 2020 for me personally as this was Jade's due date for Hugo Jaden Hart.

We are now at the end of June 2020, and I had the most amazing dream of Jade, it was amazing to see her face and smile, and I haven't dreamt about her for months. My dream was everywhere I walked, she would be walking behind me. I had to build up the strength to turn around and tell her that she had died, as she was so confused where she was and what was going on. We spoke about all that had happened, and I got an amazing hug, just what I needed due to lockdown and then she remembered around dying. I told her to start spending more time with her family, and in my dream, she said, "Yes, I want to be around Mum more." We were both standing there looking at her resting place together, talking to each other and talking about our love for each other, and she was saying, "I will never leave you." What a lovely dream to see Jade again, so I just wanted to share this with the world. What does this mean? Does this mean I've found a place in my heart of acceptance? A place many never even get to. I suppose if I find this place, it's down to all my strategies and focus around battling through terrifying times during the last two years head-on and doing it the hard way.

I also, coming out of lockdown, chose bravery and confidence, knowing that life has to go on for me and Hugo and I wasn't going to let a virus affect this. I could have quite easily fallen into major depression in lockdown and completely become a bundle of anxiety, but I found a way to stay positive and take the right direction, in my opinion, through my strategies and attitude towards life. I guess, in a nutshell, compared to what has happened to me, COVID 19 is quite small. I get there is a virus out there, and everyone's playing their part to help and support, but I needed to keep going with my normal routine and support around me to step forward. One example is I travelled to Benidorm in July with some friends, and it was well worth it, and it was a great experience to say we travelled in the heart of the pandemic, but we are all fit and well and I'm sure this will remain the case. This is an example of me choosing to live, never forget the saying, get busy living or get busy dying. I know which one I choose. If anyone is finding life hard and ever wants to talk, you know where I am or reach me through social media.

Hugo's Book *Hugo and Daddy's Night-time Adventures* was released online and published officially on Monday 12 October 2020 and has soared in sales across the country and globally too. After week two, the book got into the top 10 best sellers for its categories 2nd 4th and 6th, and I just can't believe how well it has done. I believe I played a big part in the book, as I've always been creative and an ideas guy, shooting for the stars, but all the praise goes to every single person who supported me to improve exposure of my book; so much love to everyone for this and also my illustrator, Jacqueline Tee, who brought it all to life. The best positions the book got to in its categories on best sellers on Amazon was 2nd for the category Death and Dying, 4th for Fiction Death and Dying, and 6th for General Bedtime Stories, leapfrogging *Peppa Pig*, which is insane.

I wanted to add as I write this now in November 2020, I am already creating Hugo's second book in lockdown 2, which will be released spring 2021, and this is called *Hugo and Daddy's Thailand Adventures*. The purpose of this book shows the steps and favourite islands Jade and I went to and having a vision that me and Hugo one day will do the same, and the story is told through this book. I can't wait for this one to come out, and very proud of the work, poetry and ideas around this project. Further to add to Hugo's book collection, *Hugo and Daddy's Superhero Adventures* has also been created and is focused around Hugo becoming a superhero in his own right and finding strength as a child and eating well. (A very powerful book with deep meaning.) The release date of this will be July 2021 for his third birthday.

Final Summary of the Book

In summary of all my love and heartache as mentioned above, I dealt with my anger through my running and going very long distances, which in turn created an image shift in my mind from all the trauma and heartache I had experienced into pure love and all the amazing images and expressions Jade used to make. Improving my respiratory system also helped me to work from day to day, becoming the best version of myself around Hugo. Dealing with the loss of Jade alongside always thinking of death, looking at Hugo for months, and also dealing with my own suicidal thoughts, breathing better and being in touch with nature, running moved me forward massively through my grief. Changing Jade's flowers on her grave, where it still said Pupy, every two weeks helped my heart patch up in some way as it was something to look forward to every fortnight and doing something beautiful for Jade. I also would go for Thai massages regularly, the relaxation and spa music was a huge part of mine and Jade's life, so doing this regularly took me back in my mind to our Thailand dream and again helped me in many ways.

The books have also been the missing jigsaw but now are my huge focus with amazing purpose for Hugo and Jade and also the charities I will be working with going forward. Life is about giving back now, my third rule on Ric's Rules: 1. Follow your dreams 2. Follows your passion 3. Give something back 4. Choose love and happiness. Time will not heal, love will, in my opinion.

I write my last few words of my book now, in a place I never thought I would get to (hope) and the achievements I never thought I would achieve and embracing mine and Hugo's life going forward and embracing what will come our way in life, and a new normal for me and Hugo, and starting our own journey together as he grows older. There is one thing I do believe in, though, and that's love, and I suppose I have to be open to love going forward again. Love conquers all, always has, always will.

My message to any couple out there is never grow old in your relationship and never lose sight of what brought you together from day one. Me and Jade never did and, my god, our Pupy love always stayed at 18 years old. From calling each other Pupy every day and nodding at each other as it always made everything OK. Jade sucking her thumb never moved my mind from our love at 18 years old, I guess we always spoke to each other in a way where we were still kids deep down in love, and it always remained. We had our own sign language on what meant I love you, I'm mad with you etc. I would kiss Jade 20 times a day always and tell her I loved her constantly, and this never grew old, saying it in our baby language to each other. Our communication to stay deep in love was epic and was for sure "Pupy Love".

I feel me and Hugo will have huge purpose in life, in terms of helping others in some shape or form, but I want my son to grow older, to understand a few things.

1. Always be yourself.
2. Don't let others dint your self-confidence, it's never your issues, always theirs.
3. Follow your heart.
4. Lead by example.
5. Follow your passions and be the best version of yourself.
6. Love with all your heart.

Jade, we lived one hell of a life together, and you will always be my soulmate, my Pupy, my first love, my best friend, but my journey will go on with purpose for our only son, Hugo Jaden Hart.

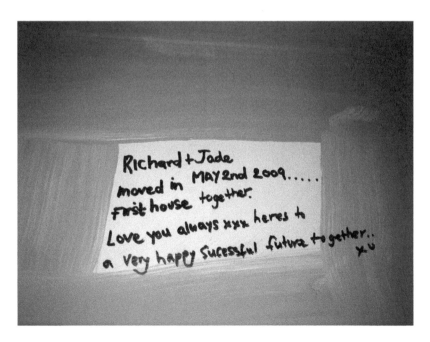

Our first date.

Memories with my Besties

I decided to do a memory chapter to share with everyone all the beautiful and funny memories that stay in all Jade's friends' hearts as most of us won't be aware of these, so I thought it was a nice touch to end the book with memories and personal messages from Jade's friends and family and my family.

Louise Moore

We had all been out in Sheffield on a Saturday. Ric, you may have met with everyone, but everyone headed back to Sarah and John's pad at the cottage. We had spoken about going to Alton Towers the next day, so we had no sleep, then we all drove to Alton Towers in Sarah's campervan, but Jade had stayed at my flat in Sheffield, near Norfolk Park. Jade text me on the Saturday morning to see if we were all going to Alton Towers. With everyone still drunk from the night before, as we all arrived in the campervan towards Sheffield, the text came in from Jade. In the haze, everyone had totally forgotten Jade had stopped at Ric's, but I text Jade back saying we will be in Sheffield in about 5 minutes. Jade came running down the Norfolk Park hill in last night's outfit, heels, fur coat, dived in the campervan. Jade went round all day at Alton Towers in last night's outfit, I just thought *You legend*, definitely a great memory.

Always a wheeler-dealer selling fags at V Festival for £5 even though she never smoked in her life and then buying a policeman's hat and wearing it with a bin bag, it was torrential rain and dancing on the picnic table.

Jade and I called each other Shelly, we could never pinpoint where the name originated from, although over the years references to the name would pop up, we somehow always found ways to link it into what we did, what we wore and even the cocktails we drank. The name just seemed to pop up when we least expected it, and it would always make us crack up laughing. Only a few years ago, we linked the name directly to Jade as her middle name is Michelle, all this time she was the original Shelly, how had we never realised?! It was a completely ridiculous ongoing 'in' joke between us that we got so much mileage out of and never failed to make us laugh.

Jade was all about the experiences in life, it was my favourite thing about her, she was always the one who showed up regardless, usually followed by her saying 'life is too short'. She was non-judgemental, always there to say exactly what you wanted to hear and made everything so much fun. We had a tradition of closing our eyes whilst doing something, dancing in Ibiza or walking down the street in Barcelona, always holding hands to hold each other up, it seems so silly to think about, but it always made sense at the time!

I feel so lucky to have had one of the last holidays with her in Turkey before Hugo was born and made memories to cherish forever. We bought overpriced fake handbags that broke once we got home, drank cheap wine all day and danced into the sunset most nights, probably had our eyes closed for the most part and screaming Shelly at any opportunity.

I love and miss you, Jade, my Shelly sister forever x

Sarah Simpson

When I used to live with my brother, we always used to have these crazy house parties and they were always brilliant, going on till like 5am in the morning and everybody would just find a place to sleep and go to sleep. We would wake up in the morning with everyone really groggy and still hungover. Jade was always the one that would go to the kitchen and start tidying up with my brother. This one time, she was doing the pots and put the washing up liquid in, and he went outside to clear some bottles, but little did he know that every time Jade would wash a pot, she would add more fairy liquid. He then came back in and Jade was in this sea of bubbles, and they had risen up all over the kitchen sides. She was such a legend, she wouldn't just turn up, get drunk and go, she was always the first one up with John and doing the tidy up. I can just see this cartoon picture surrounded in bubbles saying, 'OMG, what do I dooooo!'

Claire Davies

I have loads of memories being out with our girl who always made me smile and could out-dance the best of us! Whenever I think of Jade, the only word I can think of is 'light'. She just seemed to make everything brighter, and I was always was so happy when I knew Jade was able to come to whatever we had planned, she made things that little bit better if that makes sense...

The one memory that sticks in my mind was the last time I saw her, at Lisa and Kev's wedding reception. She was heavily pregnant and feeling a bit fed up as she couldn't really walk properly, but she was glowing and so happy. When I was leaving, I gave her a big hug and said, 'Next time I see you, you'll be a mummy,' and her face broke out into this massive smile and she said, 'I know, I just can't wait.' Hugo was so loved even before he was born xxxxx

Chantelle Williams

I have to say one of my favourite memories of Jade was her telling me she was pregnant too, and the joy on her face was priceless. Sharing the journey with her was so special, I was six weeks ahead, so we'd compare vegetable/fruit sizes our babies were supposed to be! Finding out she was also having a boy made it all the more special. What has had a lasting impression on me was the last time I saw her. The night of Lisa's home wedding party, you were picking Claire up and you both came to meet Huw. As a new mum, I was overwhelmed and making it up as I went along with no clue really as to what I was doing, he needed a change and a feed, so I went into the conservatory. As you were leaving, I was still feeding, so Jade came in to say goodbye – she kissed me on the top of my head and told me I was a natural and an earth mother. As I was feeling completely the opposite, it gave me confidence and trust in my abilities even after we'd lost her and I sunk into a bit of a depression, her words lifted me up and made me carry on. She always knew just what to say to make everything better, and I thank her for those words, which saw me through some difficult times.

Natalie Irvine

It was my first girls' holiday to Malia, and I heard that Tania had a uni friend joining us. I remember sunbathing on the beach and seeing this beautiful girl wearing only a thong bikini bottom. I asked the girls, 'Who is that girl in the thong?' 'That's Tania's friend from uni. Jade,' they replied. I remember thinking *WOW she's beautiful* and just being in complete awe of her before we had even spoken.

We chatted a bit on the beach, her personality was just infectious. I was desperate to be her friend. I didn't need to try hard; she was the easiest person I have ever met to become friends with almost overnight. We used to say we were sisters. We made lots of plans on the holiday to keep in touch when we returned to the UK. And we did. I arrived back in England and made my way to the first of many trips to Birmingham that same weekend. The rest is history.

We shared 14 years of friendship, there was so much dancing (especially table dancing), laughing, trips away, shopping, phone calls that went on for hours, I spoke to her on the car phone once almost the entire way between Sheffield and Glasgow!

There were many times in our friendships that her amazingness blew me away. My wedding day was one of them. Mine and my husband's family had never met, and Jade knew how nervous I was about this happening on the night before the wedding. I will never forget at the pre-wedding dinner, Jade taking a large drink of her prosecco and saying, "Right, I'm off to mingle." And off she went, introducing herself to both sides of the family. I knew then that the evening would go great as Jade made her way around the guests making sure everyone was happy and having fun. On the wedding day she wore a dress that was made of feathers from the waist down, god she looked great in that dress.

Rohanna Griffin

The first time I met Jade, she was in our halls of residence. She was dressed in the most ridiculous but gorgeous outfit of a teeny tiny denim skirt. She had cut it into what looked like a belt and used the cut-off part as a choker around her neck. She was plastered in makeup and was dancing on a chair to Peaches banging on the ceiling. She made an impact and always owned a room; albeit unintentionally. She was also the sweetest, kindest girl I was ever lucky enough to meet. From buying me tickets to a concert she couldn't attend to help me through heartache, to encouraging me to stay at uni when I wanted to leave, Jade always made me feel special and valued. Me, Tania and Jade used to call ourselves the tripod and said we couldn't stand up without each other. We were each other's left and right legs. Best friends for life.

We had the best holidays... One memory in particular was our cava-fuelled trip to Barcelona with myself, Jade, Louise and Shona. We indulged in great food and drink at trendy spots around the city. One day to get over our hangovers, we decided that 'hair of the dog' was the best option. We drank bubbles in the park with the sun blazing down on us and before visiting Gaudi's Sagrada Familia. It was not the most appropriate moment to attend a holy building whilst giddy, but it was beautiful and hilarious all at the same time! I've never laughed so much.

We also had a couple of amazing trips to Ibiza, Jade's favourite party destination. One of the highlights of a trip was going to see Swedish House Mafia at Ushuaia, with Kirsty too. We partied all day and ended the gig by all jumping fully clothed into the swimming pool. It was a brilliant moment, having been told not to do it, we thought we would do it anyway – it was such a rush, and I will never forget how it felt to be together.

From our first day at uni, our worldwide adventures, her dream wedding in Thailand to telling me about her pregnancy, we were always together, and I will never forget her smile and the sunbeams that constantly glowed from her face. The purest and kindest of hearts, Mrs Jade Michelle Hart will be in mine forever.

Tania Dean

I have so many special memories with Jade. She brought love, light, happiness and laughs into all of our lives, and I will cherish every moment forever.

One memory that really makes me smile is when we went to Wales for Seren's christening. On the way home, Ric stopped the car as there was a horse and its gorgeous little foal in a field. We were there for quite a while looking at how cute they were. Jade was taking lots of photos. When we got back into the car, I was excited to see what she had caught on camera and said, 'Ahhh, Jade, I bet you got some amazing shots.' When she presented us with the photos, we were in stitches, and we have never laughed so much in our lives! It was half of the foal's head and the mummy horse's backside. I remember her laugh; it was so infectious.

Myself, Jade and Ro have been best friends since the beginning of uni. After our travel trip that started off in Australia together, that took us all in various directions, we all settled back in England in separate nearby towns. Myself and Jade used to visit Ro in Matlock quite often. One morning we woke up feeling quite hungover after a boozy night out. Jade was always so kind and thoughtful, and she had offered to drive me to a christening in Maltby, as it was over one hour away, and public transport would've been near impossible. Jade asked to borrow some tights and Ro brought down the only clean ones she had – the brightest blue tights I had ever seen! They were the colour of a Smurf. Only our Jade could pull them off. We set off that morning with Jade driving a slow, overly cautious 30mph on the motorway in the middle lane. We were both tired and laughing. Jade said, 'I hope the fashion police don't pull me over for wearing these tights,' and we laughed some more. She dropped me off right at the door and made sure I was safe.

Jade was the most amazing best friend and I feel honoured to be one hers. Jade will always be the core to our circle of girlfriends, the heart that binds us all forever. Jade, I will always take you with me in everything I do and channel your positive energy.

Lisa Homar

I can't say this about many people, but I remember the moment I met Jade for the very first time, which I can only put down to her making such a huge impression and me instantly knowing we'd be lifelong friends.

We took an impromptu girls' trip to Blackpool to celebrate Nat's birthday back in 2005. Tan brought her uni friend along, who everyone assured me 'You're gonna absolutely love!' and they weren't wrong! She had me laughing instantly when she clipped into her hair Lindsey's brand-new extensions (totally the wrong colour for Jade) but she wanted to wear them anyway. Thankfully, Lindsey managed to talk her out of it. Jade was more full of life than anyone I had ever met, and the smile never left her face all day. I'm sure Jade was the instigator for us all rocking Spice Girls on a karaoke, and she was definitely the first one up on a table dancing – I don't think I'd ever danced on a table before I met Jade! Later that day, we really bonded over a pot of garlic mayo, which I said she could have when she started scooping it out with her fingers, having the most lovely chat about everything, in particular how we both had a passion for spirituality. I have since had some of the best times of my life with Jade, whether they be the biggest laughs on nights out, or our quiet chats that I never wanted to end!

Throughout our friendship, Jade has given me the courage to do so many things I may have shied away from. Jade would tell me stories of how she'd done or said something silly in an important meeting at work but was able to view this positively and laugh at herself. Jade's outlook and positivity have had such an impact on me as a person, I admire her more than I can say. So often I think 'what would Jade do/feel?' then I do as I intended and always look on the bright side. She inspires me to be proud of being me – such a special quality to find in a person.

The memory of Jade that I hold closest to my heart is from my hen do in Paris in May 2018, which Jade so kindly helped Lou to organise. She knew how much I loved Paris and wanted to share it with my friends. I once told her about a grate outside the Moulin Rouge and how it's my dream to have a photo with my friends there. Being such a kind-hearted person, Jade remembered this, and on the night, we went to see the show and were stood outside near the grate having a group photo, she waited for a clear in the crowds of people then ran and leaped up onto it. She told me how no matter how embarrassed we were that everyone was looking, we had to have a photo together on it and I couldn't let her down. I unwillingly climbed up and we hugged. As Louise took the photo, Jade whispered in my ear, 'Happy hen do, I love you.' That was one of the most incredible moments of my life. I knew how unbelievably lucky I was to have such an amazing friend that could make me feel so special. She made a dream of mine come true that night, and I will never forget how she made me feel for the rest of my life.

Shona Jefferson

Hello Hugo!!

So, your amazing dad has asked me to put pen to paper to tell you of a few fond memories or funny stories I have of your mummy so that you can grow to know a little about us as friends and what a kind, dizzy, thoughtful, funny and incredibly special friend your mum was to me and all of us girls.

Now this comes with a warning, your Auntie Sho could write a book... I wasn't named JK Rowling by your mummy and friends for no reason!

THE HART OF OUR CIRCLE

It was a Monday; I was working from home and knew it was the week you would arrive. For some reason, I knew I needed to see Jade on this day. We arranged that I would drive up for some dinner and sit and catch up in the garden. Ric made us a healthy dinner of sweet potatoes and salad. Jade ate with her fingers; she always did this!

Jade was wearing a yellow floral dress. One of her mum's dresses, and she laughed that she hadn't taken it off in weeks! She looked so beautiful pregnant, her hair in her trademark knotted bun and her skin glowing in the evening sunlight.

Jade spoke of how happy she felt that Ric was now self-employed and how grateful she was that he had been working from home for the duration of her pregnancy. She spoke of Ric making her pancakes for breakfast, long walks along the canal and brunches at The Pantry.

The healthy dinner is key to this memory as Jade and I had always been a bad influence on each other when it came to snacks! I was trying to be healthy, which was soon forgotten when Jade came back from the kitchen with a packet of Blue Ribbons. Only 98cals, she said. Within minutes we had eaten the entire packet of 8... We laughed hard that they were like air and we hadn't even tasted them!

Before heading home, Jade was eager to show me the contents of your baby bag, all packed and ready for you to arrive. A Cath

Kidston baby bag stuffed full of hand-knitted cardigans and hats, but the item I remember most was the outfit your Nana Julie had bought from Lincoln – the outfit she told me she wanted you to wear first.

She asked me to braid her hair like we were at a festival again, only this time for the hospital. She loved me plaiting her hair, and I loved doing something that made her feel so happy.

Jade lived her life for creating magical memories with the people she loved most.

I am so grateful for this memory and will forever be my most cherished.

Tea Trays and Crystal – Jade and I started our friendship through work. Firstly, at Karen Millen when she was at uni and I was a second-time mum returning to work. Regardless of how different our lives were, we instantly became close friends, sharing the same work ethic and dreaming of owning a shop together, travelling the world as buyers.

Jade and I did some time apart whilst she worked at Whistles and I studied fashion, but our friendship always remained strong. Years later, we went on to work together again at Springboard. We spoke every day, often for hours in the car, stayed in boutique hotels together and partied hard at a lot of industry events! It was a year when we had been snowed in, it was really deep and not safe on the roads. A Wednesday, I think, and we would work from home the next day. I shouldn't have driven, but we planned that I would hit the M1 and come and stay with Jade and Ric.

We got tipsy and decided we would go sledging in the snow… We didn't have a sledge, so we strapped tea trays to our feet as skis and headed for a big hill near the Manor. We laughed so much and didn't get very far before being forced to ditch the tea trays! When we reached the hill, we found an abandoned wheelie bin lid and Property for Sale sign that we quickly claimed as our own so that we could sledge the slope. It was freezing, we were inappropriately dressed but we had the best time fooling around in the dark, hitting bumps and rolling down the hill. As with most nights we were together, we decided that even though the roads were shin-high in snow, we would head home, change and head out to Crystal for a night out!

We had so many great nights out together!

The day Jade showed me her wedding dress we were in the flat, I can't remember who was there, but I remember Jade had been to a wedding show and had chosen her dress. She was beaming with joy and so happy that she had found the most perfect dress. I was probing for a description, and she said that she had some photos of her in it and did I want to see? This was a tough decision because I was desperate to see but also told her I never wanted her to show me because I wanted to wait until I saw her on her special day... I crumbled, I couldn't wait!

She pulled out an iPad, asked me to close my eyes then put the iPad in my hand... I opened my eyes and remember feeling incredibly overwhelmed. I burst into tears and have never felt so happy! She looked beyond beautiful and so classy... Her dark hair in a middle parting, swept back into a low bun. She looked so regal like the princess Kate Middleton on her wedding day! It was everything that I wanted for her and was overcome with emotion. Jade squealed in excitement, eyes streaming the happiest of tears. She said my reaction was exactly what she needed to see to confirm she had found 'The Dress'. This will always be such a special memory for me because of how much she valued my opinion and how happy my reaction made her feel.

Fast forward to Thailand... one of the highlights of my life.

Not only do I feel blessed to have spontaneously booked last minute with Louise to travel together to see our best friend marry her soulmate and Pupy, Ric, but to be asked to do Jade's makeup and Louise her nails was an honour. Again, this memory so special and etched deep into my heart. I love you so much, Jade, and not a single day passes without you in my thoughts.

Life is not the same without you in it, I am not the person I once was, but I promise to live life gratefully, stay positive and keep making magical memories – You taught me this! Your legacy lives on in the lives of everyone you touched.

Rachel Jones

Some of my most beautiful memories of Jade are from the summer of 2003 when we packed our bags and flew off to Kardamena on the Greek Island of Kos for the summer.

We sold our worldly possessions to buy a one-way plane ticket, and a week on an 18–30's holiday, and away we flew without a care or responsibility in the world.

We went out searching for jobs and were quickly offered them as barmaids or waitresses, only to be fired as quickly as we started. We were hopeless. We got too drunk, our clothes were too revealing, we were always late, and we talked too much. Generally, we were way more interested in having fun together than doing the job we were paid to do, and we were genuinely shocked every time our employer caught on and let us go.

Eventually though, we found the one, Ultramarine Bar, being paid to chat to passing holidaymakers and get them in for a drink. We were made for the job.

We made so many amazing friends; locals, other Brits working for the summer, holidaymakers that became our instant new best friends… for a week, before they went home, and the next group arrived.

We were paid to party, drunk our body weight in vodka and orange every night, and danced until the sun came up every morning.

In the daytimes, we sat in our favourite bars watching non-stop episodes of *Friends* for six hours straight. We shared a family size shepherd's pie and HP sauce at our favourite café Lazy Daze… every day that we could afford to eat.

We got an apartment and decorated it with Jade's colourful scarves and photos of our family and friends from home, a (very messy) place to call home. We sunbathed on the roof in nothing but our thongs and baby oil. We adopted kittens, dogs and goats. We rode our bikes everywhere and fell off when we were too drunk or hungover to remember how to ride.

We had too many adventures, dramas, romances and hilarious moments to count. We looked out for each other no matter what, spent every minute of every day together and never had a cross word. We made each other laugh like nobody else could.

It was a summer of true friendship that I'll cherish for the rest of my life.

Lindsey Dziendziel

Jade was the most beautiful soul I have ever met, even to this day. So positive, loving, caring and thoughtful. Always having time for everyone and gave herself 100% to you when you were with her. She had the ability to see good in everything. And Jade knew how to have fun. First time on holiday with Jade, I thought *Wow, just what a babe*. This tall, beautiful girl with amazing little figure that could completely carry off a thong bikini strutting her stuff around Malia.

We fancied breakfast one morning so off we went to a greasy spoon for an English breakfast, and I was amazed that Jade managed to eat the whole thing, without even using cutlery. Always made me laugh. And her love of mixed combination food she would have with Ric, e.g., sausage surprise, the surprise was there was no sausage. Thank you for being you, Jade.

Kirsty Walker (Jade's Cousin)

One of my favourite memories of us both was in July 2012, Jade surprised me with VIP tickets to see Swedish House Mafia's final concert at Milton Keynes. Walking round in our matching bowler hats, I'll never forgot someone approached Jade saying he was sure he had seen her on television before. Jade replied, 'Yes, you have, we was on X Factor last year (2011) we are Two Shoes.'

The guy looked shocked and said, 'Yes, you are,' shouting his family and friends over. Jade stood there having photos, I couldn't actually believe they had believed her. She called me over whispering in my ear, 'Come on, Kirst, pose. They think we are famous.' I never felt so embarrassed but still joining her. She just didn't care; she was loving it. We walked off laughing our heads off that they believed us.

The whole concert we never moved from the front, dancing the whole night away. The concert we were at was in their music video to the single 'Don't You Worry Child'. So, we got our fame that night after all. Amazing memories.

My second favourite memory has to Thailand.

Jade and Ric's wedding day. Jade turned to me on the beach and said, 'We have a surprise; don't scream.' I replied, 'Is Olly Murs here?' Jade said, 'No, an elephant.' We laughed so much, big difference, but someone actually caught the moment of our faces on camera. Walking up the beach came an elephant attending their wedding. A wedding so perfect in every single way.

It was mind-blowing. I am forever thankful to share this experience.

Jade, in a world where we have a lifetime of memories together, it was so hard to pick a couple out. A massive part of my life, in your company was always such the best times from holidays to days/nights out, concerts, sleepovers, spa days and much more. Life is just not the same without you. The most beautiful person I've ever met inside and out. A massive hole you have left in many of our hearts. I am forever grateful for the memories I have, and you will forever live on. Love you always. My other shoe xx

Jade's Family

I also wanted to add in Jade's immediate family and end the book this way also with my family, so here are some special memories and images at the back of Jade's family members' and mine memories that stay close to their heart, and also personal messages.

John Hazelgrave

I have lots of lovely memories of spending time with Jade, she loved music, like me, and in the year 2000 when she was 15 years old, we went to the Glastonbury Festival. I took her right to the front and she watched David Bowie on my shoulders. This was a special time for both of us and one that I will never forget.

Another special memory is when we went as a family to Las Vegas for my 60th birthday. When we arrived, she popped out the 60th decorations and a surprise limousine arrived, me and my wife renewed our vows after 38 years, and we went on a helicopter over the Grand Canyon. We had an amazing time as a family and was a very special holiday, I will never forget.

My proudest moment with Jade was the day she got married in Thailand. She looked so beautiful and happy. Her last words before we walked down the aisle were, 'Let's do it, Dad.' We both felt so happy, emotional, and nervous.

I really miss and love Jade so much. 'Wish you were here' (Pink Floyd).

Love Dad x

Julie Hazelgrave

A special memory of Jade is the day she was born, 15th August 1984. We were thrilled to bits with her and loved her so much from the moment she arrived. She was a mischievous baby, had the terrible twos at 18 months old. When she was 15, she thought she was 21. She kept us on our toes, but she grew up into a beautiful young woman, full of life, who loved adventure and travel.

We were proud of all Jade's educational achievements and were bursting with pride at her graduation.

Jade had a knack of being able to make you feel special, she would go out of her way to celebrate birthdays and anniversaries making each and every one memorable.

My proudest and most special time is when she delivered hers and Ric's beautiful son, Hugo. She was the happiest I had seen her at that moment, saying his skin was so soft and she couldn't believe he was hers. I kissed her several times on her cheek and left her and Ric to bond with their new little family. As I left the room, I looked back from the doorway, seeing Jade holding Hugo. I felt so relieved, proud and happy and very emotional. This is the last time I saw Jade and is a moment I will remember forever.

Thank you, Jade, for your special and precious gift of Hugo, our first grandchild. Thank you for all our lovely and special memories together. I know you loved us, just as much as we love you.

Love Mum x

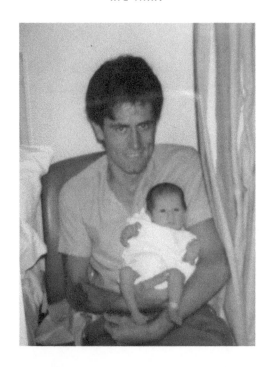

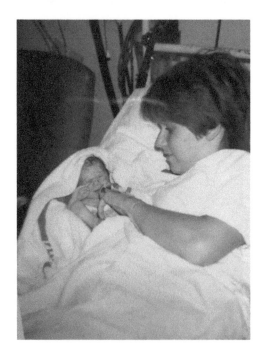

Daniel Hazelgrave

Dear Jade,

I have been asked to write down some memories of you as we were children and growing up together but where do I begin? There are too many and they would fill a library. I have decided to pick some that stand out to me the most. We would play, laugh and fight like most siblings would and in the beginning, it was just the two of us before Sally came. You used to be naughty and I suppose we egged each other on. When Sally came, we used to take great delight in scaring her by telling her the stems and leaves on top of tomatoes were spiders. She would believe us so we would throw them at her until she ran away crying! Quite mean really looking back but that's what siblings do, taunt each other. As we grew up and went off to school, we found other friends and went off on our own separate journeys. But, on a Tuesday we would love going to Granny Joan's for our tea after school where she would do us an enormous Sunday dinner, enough food for 10 sometimes and there were only three of us! I suppose we grew further apart and did our own thing as you went to university in Birmingham and then went on your epic journey travelling to the far east and Australia. But we always got together for important occasions, and it was like we were never apart. On one occasion, you had made a wedding dress for a university project, which worked great for me too as I did a photoshoot of you (which in turn helped me with a college photography project). We spent the day in the college studio, relaxed, taking pictures, messing around and just enjoying each other's company. I think you knew that I like to keep myself to myself and don't like a lot of fuss. But that never meant (and still doesn't) that I don't care about the most important things in life. I could go on and on, but I think I will end this passage with my very last couple of memories of you. When I saw you walking down the garden path at Sally's 30th birthday in your long flowing dress, I thought that you looked really beautiful and blooming, ready to welcome your new baby into your life. I also remember me, you and Daniela sitting in the dining room together, when you all of sudden grabbed Daniela's hand to put to your stomach as the baby was moving. This was a touching moment; I think you loved your sister-in-law Daniela and most people who touched your life. My very last memory is when we all went out for a meal to George's restaurant in Leeds. You looked a little fed up, I suppose because it was very hot that day. But we had a lovely photo together. Me, you and Sally. You asked for a small portion of food while rubbing your stomach and telling the waitress "There isn't much room in here". I smiled at that, and when we finished our meal, I gave you a big hug and kiss, as me and Daniela would be on holiday when you would be having your baby. I said I was looking forward to coming back and seeing you and my new nephew. However, in hindsight this was never meant to be. So, all I have left to say is I love you forever and always and, I know this is a cliché, but you *are* always in my heart.

Your Brother,
Daniel

Daniela Hazelgrave

Doncaster St Leger Festival 2014

On the 13th September 2014, we all went to the Doncaster St Leger festival, for John's 57th birthday. Before we went into the racecourse, we all met up at the St Leger Hotel for a couple of drinks. It was absolutely heaving everywhere, as is the case for one of the most prestigious racehorse meets of the year! We finished our drinks and entered the grandstand where we decided to do an impromptu "photo shoot". Myself, Jade and Daniel were messing around posing for 'selfies' when we erupted into a fit of giggles. It must have been the few wines we quickly drank before we got in, plus the excitement of the day ahead! Me and Jade sang 'Wasted' by ZHU, a dance song she loved from when she visited Ibiza. We all had a brilliant day and had plenty of winners. Jade was flitting from the grandstand to the county stand as that's where Ric was most of the day. Upon her return(s) she would have something in her hands, one time was a pork sandwich for herself and the next, a bag of flip flops which were much appreciated, due to the aching of the girls' feet from being in high heels all day! After the racing had come to a close, we moved inside the grandstand where a band was playing. We were all quite inebriated by this stage, but the music kept us going. Jade danced and twirled with her dad, John, as she loved to do. That is until the twirling got a bit much and John found himself on the floor, much to the security man's amusement. After this was the debate of where we should go to eat, some wanted Italian, some wanted Indian. In the end, an Indian restaurant called Shabirs was chosen in Doncaster city centre. After we ate came the usual "we're going to go and get some more drinks in town" statement from some of the 'boys'.

This was never going to happen as most people had had more than enough to drink by this point. So, Jade and Ric had to spend some of their winnings on a taxi fare back to Sheffield, which ended up being around £60. All in all, I am writing this to share one of many wonderful memories of our dear Jade. I chose this occasion as it was a joyous time, and all of her close immediate family were there to celebrate her dad's birthday. Of course, there will have been some hangovers the next day!

We love and miss you always, Jade, your brother Daniel and sister-in-law Daniela.

Rob Hammond

I was fortunate to have met Jade through my wife and have such a great sister-in-law and friend. We spent a lot of time together as a group of four and also Jade would regularly come and spend time at our house during the week, spending many an evening having dinner together. In terms of memories, I have one special day that sticks out for me amongst hundreds of others. In 2017, Jade, Sally, Ric and I went on the trip of a lifetime to Thailand touring around. Songkran that year fell on a day when we were on our favourite island, Koh Lipe. We had such a great day, drinking, having water fights, finishing up in a beach club to see the night out. The reason it sticks out so much was just the pure zest for life

Jade had, and it warms my heart thinking back to how much fun she had that day with a smile beaming continuously. Jade, you were a special person, someone who I loved spending time with and a person who just made everything that bit more special. Love you, Rob XxX

Sally Hammond

I have so many special memories of Jade as I was growing up. She wasn't just my sister; she was my best friend. I was so lucky to have this relationship with her, that so many will never experience. She made everything special for me, to my birthdays, our amazing holidays, my hen parties and making my wedding an amazing day. My mum, Jade and I had such a special bond and would do most things together, we had many spa days, afternoon teas and cocktail afternoons.

We travelled so much together, and our favourite destination was Thailand. When we arrived on an island called Ko Rok Noi, we thought we had arrived in paradise. We went into the clear, blue sea and sent video messages to all of our family to wish them Happy Easter from a piece of heaven. I have not been anywhere that compares to this and will treasure this memory forever.

She was the best maid of honour, and when my wedding sandals broke just before we went down the aisle, she gave me hers and walked down barefooted, she helped me to go to the toilet, topped my make-up throughout the day and danced with me on the table until it collapsed. At Jade's wedding, we felt like movie stars, and I remember dancing with her on the beach and she said she was the happiest she had ever been.

Jade, I love you so much.

Sally

Shirley Medlock (Jades Nan)

I have so many precious memories of my very first grandchild, Jade.

I loved her from the time she was born and as she grew was the cutest baby with a cheeky little character. As Jade got older, she gave so much joy to me and her grandad and we adored her.

Particular times are memorable to me; one was Jade graduating from the University of Central England in Birmingham, she was my star then! The graduation evening when presented with her degree, I felt immense pride in her she had done so well.

Another important time – well for Jade! – was her decision to go travelling with friends, which turned out to be as far New Zealand with other countries visited along the way, some part was on her own when others stayed places longer. This is when I feared for her so far away and for so long, but she joined me up on Facebook so that I could be in contact at all times, this is how thoughtful Jade was, trying to alleviate my anxiety, which I did appreciate.

I thought she was very brave committing to such a venture, but Jade was strong and determined, no doubt her friendly and kind personality with amazing strength of character helped her along and brought her back safely, but I met her in London on her return with relief and joy, I have to say, but she had enjoyed the experience.

Finally, my memory is of the amazing wedding in Jade's favourite place, Thailand.

Jade made the most beautiful bride, in my mind's eye I can see her now coming down the petal-strewn beach in the sun, smiling though emotional and a wee bit nervous on her dad's arm to meet up and marry Richard, the love of her life, to become Mrs Hart. She was so happy, and it was very touching to witness, and my heart was full of love for her.

My last precious memory is when Jade became mother to her much-loved baby boy, hers and Richard's amazing son, Hugo. This made me a first time very proud great-grandmother thanks to mummy Jade, and I love her son like I loved Jade; he is part of her.

So, my precious Jade, perfect in every way... So kind and considerate, always generous to a fault, had sunshine in her every smile, vivacious, full of life and so beautiful.

Me and Jade had so much love for each other and she made my life that much better for being in it.

Your Nan (Nany as you liked to call me)

I will love you forever xxx

Kim Medlock (Aunty Kim)

I have many lovely memories of Jade growing up and of her legendary kindness, generosity and thoughtfulness in adulthood; yet I'm drawn to start at the beginning. It was in my sister's house shortly after Jade had been born that I excitedly met Jade for the first time. She had the sweetest little face and nose and was such a contented baby and bundle of joy. I remember laying Jade on the bed on her side and, lying on my side also, I directly faced her and looked into her eyes. It was an unconditional and unending love from that moment.

Other special memories include the day I had the honour of becoming Jade's godmother at Jade's christening, and how, many years later, Jade in turn supported me when I was baptised as an adult in Haven Green Church, Ealing. Jade came with me, waiting with towels in hand, as I emerged from the water. As life came full circle, my love for Jade was reciprocated, and I knew I could always rely on Jade and her support of me.

My Family

Andy & Tracy Hart

We had to think long and hard about what were our favourite memories of Jade, simply because there are so many to choose from – so many days at the races, nights out, and summer BBQs to remember fondly. Our first is a funny one from New Year 2016. We woke up after a night out in Retford and Jade had the fab idea of us all having a weigh-in to set some goals for the year ahead. Upon getting the scales out, both Ric and Jade had hilarious reactions to how much weight they'd gained since their wedding in Thailand – we were howling with laughter after they'd both said they'd put on a couple of pounds whereas in reality it was actually a matter of stones!! Jade kept saying she didn't know how it was possible and told Ric they were going to have to put a fitness plan into place. We just always remember Jade's shock and how funny it was after she had been the one to suggest the weigh-in and the rest of us had only gained a few pounds!

Our second pick was Jade's reaction to us getting engaged in NYC in 2017 – we facetimed Ric, and when Andy told him the news, there was a scream from the background, and suddenly Jade shot onto the screen with a towel on her head grinning and congratulating us! It was without a doubt the best and most enthusiastic reaction to our engagement we got from anyone and is simply a reflection of the kind, positive, loving person Jade was. She immediately started asking a thousand questions wanting to know all about what had happened, our wedding plans and saying how excited she was to have a fellow Mrs Hart.

We miss you so much, Jade, and can't wait to tell our very own Baby Hart all about how amazing his Auntie Jade was,

Love always, Andy & Tracy

Sue Guy

We were at one of my other sons' wedding, in the afternoon break, my mum and I returned to our room. It was lovely and warm as this was a December wedding. We were relaxing on our beds when there was a knock at our door. Stood in front of me was Jade and Rick. We are tired and cold; our hotel is too far away. So, they came in our room. Jade said to me, "Sue, can I get in your bed with you…?" and she did. Rick sat in the comfy chair and they both went to sleep… Bless them, my mum said.

When in Thailand for the wedding, I spent some time with Jade and Rick, in Lamai (prior to their wedding). Jade took me for a midnight foot massage… we giggled so much, Rick was out drinking with friends. We returned to their beach hut, Jade and I got into bed, their queen-size bed. We chatted until we dozed off to sleep. I had such a closeness with Jade.

These memories are so special to me, although I have so many. I couldn't have asked for a better relationship with my daughter-in-law Jade, I love and miss her lust for life. I cherish all the memories that she has left me. But most of all for loving my son Rick and making him so incredibly happy. They completed each other, true soulmates.

Alanna Hart

So one of my special memories of Jade was when we were on a night out in Sheffield and we were walking to another pub, and she said I have something to ask you. Will you be my bridesmaid? I was in total shock as never expected this, and I was so happy and excited to reply with a massive Yes. The smile on my face surely said it all. Jade always made me feel close to her, just like a sister should.

The next memory always makes me giggle. So, I had gone to visit Jade and Ric, and she was telling me she had gone out with the girls and Ric had gone out with his pals, and he called her saying I'm a mouse, but the way she was telling the story with her cute expression, I was in fits of giggles and the funny memory will never leave me.

Jason Hart & Christy

One significant memory for me was playing a huge part in the amazing Thailand wedding in 2015, being best man for Ric – what an honour that was and gaining an amazing sister-in-law in Jade.

My second memory was meeting up on Phi Phi island a few nights before the big day and having a night out, me and Christy, Ric and Jade, we had a bit of food then onto the beach party for plenty of beers!! This resulted in myself being so hungover the following day on an organised day trip to one of the most beautiful islands – Maya Bay! What a fantastic night we had the four of us, I remember Jade trying to get Ric on the 'taxi boat' back to their apartment... was so funny, pretty sure Ric wanted to swim back but Jade being the sensible, calm one managed to get him on board.. literally! Memories to be treasured and ones I'll never forget.

My Final Words

Your heart and soul will live on through mine and Hugo's, our only son, and I will make you proud, Jade, I promise you this, and I feel I am doing this already. A true angel that created so much light in everyone's life and will never be forgotten. So many find it hard to talk about loved ones lost, but Jade and all I have built and created will always remain in our everyday lives for both me and Hugo. Jade lives on in our hearts and our everyday discussions and for sure mine and Hugo's baby talk to each other every day in the house and at night.

I also wanted to thank everyone for their own personal messages, Jade's closest friends and also Jade's family and my family; it means the world. And also, a thank you from me to all those who have helped me during the last two years, you know who you are. I am profoundly grateful for everything everyone has done for me and Hugo to support us. Fly high, my Jade, go to our special place, until we meet again.

Love you, miss you. Bye...

What should have been...

Lightning Source UK Ltd.
Milton Keynes UK
UKHW020649260221
379427UK00007B/152